MOUNT ST. HELENS PATHWAYS TO DISCOVERY

The Complete Visitor Guide to America's Favorite Volcano

By David H. Seesholtz

A PLUS IMAGES
4519 NE 49th St.
Vancouver, Washington 98661

MOUNT ST. HELENS, Pathways to Discovery

The Complete Visitor Guide to America's Favorite Volcano

By David H. Seesholtz

Published by:

A PLUS IMAGES
4519 NE 49th Street
Vancouver, WA 98661

Copyright © 1993 by David H. Seesholtz
Printed in the United States of America
All photos are by the author except as otherwise noted.

Library of Congress Cataloging in Publication Data
Library of Congress Catalog Card Number: 93-90139
Seesholtz, David H.
Mount St. Helens, Pathways to Discovery: The Complete Visitor Guide to America's Favorite Volcano by David H. Seesholtz

Includes index, bibliography, maps and photographs
ISBN 0-9636168-0-3
1. Mount St. Helens National Volcanic Monument-Trails, 2. Mount St. Helens-Description and Travel, 3. Mountain biking-Mount St. Helens, 4. Hiking-Mount St. Helens-Guide books, 5. Horse riding-Mount St. Helens

Cover photo: Hiker on Harmony Falls Trail at Spirit Lake.

To all the Interpreters and other employees of the Gifford Pinchot National Forest and specifically the Mount St. Helens National Volcanic Monument who have been steadfast in their efforts to reveal the truths that lie behind this unusual landscape.

and

To the memory of my special friend and colleague, Wayne Parsons, who played a major role in planning and rebuilding these recreation opportunities that we will enjoy for many years.

The author and Queen at his favorite viewpoint on Mt. Margaret Ridge in 1976. Photo by Wayne Parsons.

About The Author

When David Seesholtz moved to the St. Helens Ranger District of the Gifford Pinchot National Forest in 1973, he was unaware of the change that would occur to his Forest Service career and to the rest of his life. As the Resource Forester responsible for planning and managing the recreation around Spirit Lake and Mount St. Helens, he had no idea of the world class volcanic event that would occur here in May 1980. When the mountain began reawakening in March of 1980, Dave was responsible for writing the contingency plan for the ranger district and led the evacuation of the ranger station. Later his duties included providing opportunities for both the public and the media to experience what was happening here.

Dave had always been interested in interpreting the environment into easily understood language and to stimulate visitors into wanting to know more about the forest. His interpretive skills were called upon for building and operating the first visitor centers that served millions of visitors wanting to learn about the volcano. In 1983 he became the principle outdoor recreation planner and co-author of the Comprehensive Management Plan for the Mount St. Helens National Volcanic Monument.

An avid outdoorsman, he has packed his camera over most of the 110,300 acres of the National Volcanic Monument and surrounding landscape while planning and building the new recreation facilities. He is excited about sharing his photographs with you and sharing with you his inside information on how to have a great experience during your visit.

In 1991, Dave retired after a 33 year career with the Forest Service in the Pacific Northwest Region. A life long photographer, he has now started a new career as a free-lance writer and photographer in Vancouver, WA under the name, "A Plus Images". Many of his photographs have appeared in Forest Service documents, audio-visual programs, and displays.

Dave, a native of Reading, PA, was prompted to write this book because many of his friends and colleagues approached him to share some of his inside information on where these roads, trails, and other facilities are located, and how they could enhance a visit to the area. They were familiar with his expertise on the new facilities at the monument and the lack of up-to-date guide books. He is presently writing his next book, "Southwest Washington, Pathways to Discovery".

Acknowledgements

Scores of people contributed to this first complete visitor guide book for the Mount St. Helens National Volcanic Monument. Information on trail locations, uses, and distances was provided by Jim Slagle, Larry Schumacher, Jim Nieland, Walt Doan, Dave Olson, and Lori Bisconer, and information on interpretive services was provided by Jim Gale, Celese Brune, Jim Quiring, and Bonnie Lippitt all of the Gifford Pinchot National Forest. Information on geology was supplied by the U.S. Geological Survey.

Special thanks to Jim Slagle, forest trails engineer, Jim Nieland, the Monument trail manager, and Bonnie Lippitt, visitor center director, for editing for technical accuracy. Special thanks to my wife, Bonnie, for her copy editing.

I sincerely thank all these fine people. I know they are proud to have helped you in your enjoyment of this unique Monument.

Help us keep this guide up to date

In the volcanic landscape around Mount St. Helens, things change so rapidly that it's impossible for one person to keep up with everything that's happening. The 1980 eruptions destroyed most of the road and trail access into the area and new facilities are being completed every year. Your input will help us identify inaccuracies, new information, and misleading suggestions. Please write to us to let us know how we can improve this travel guide.

We especially would like new information on new discoveries that you have made. We also would appreciate hearing from food and lodging providers wishing to accommodate visitors to the area.

We are concerned about the fragility of this wonderful resource and want to continue to motivate our readers to respect and protect it. Your help in doing this would be appreciated.

Preface

The May 18, 1980 eruption of Mount St. Helens was the most awesome sight of my life. The hugh column of ash rose to an altitude of over 12 miles above the volcano. From our vantage point at Yale Reservoir about 20 miles from the mountain everything seemed to be in slow motion because of the scale. Even at that distance the wide angle lens on my camera didn't seem adequate to capture what I was seeing. It was out of scale with any thing I had ever experienced or imagined.

The volcano continued to blow ash into the giant column for over nine hours. The winds drove the ash to the east, changing day to night in the communities along its route. I have seen movies of atomic blasts, but the explosive eruption here made those images pale in comparison.

When the ash settled and we were able to take our first look at the area we were astonished at the change in the landscape. A lateral blast of hot gases, rocks and ash had devastated an area of about 230 sq. miles north of the crater in an arch of nearly 180 degrees.

In August 1982 the President signed an Act creating a 110,000 acre National Volcanic Monument. The Gifford Pinchot National Forest in partnership with the State of Washington and Cowlitz County has been building new pathways into this unique area. You are invited to drive these pathways to visitor centers and viewpoints, and discover through interpretive signs and programs that the earth is alive and constantly changing. Then walk or ride your horse or mountain bike on pathways through this changing landscape.

This is a great place to take a little time to examine the broader concepts of this dynamic planet, Earth. Visit the Mount St. Helens Visitor Center at Silver Lake, five miles east of Castle Rock first and study the information on continental drift and plate tectonics. Then as you follow the pathways through the Monument take time to ponder the creative process at work. Perhaps you'll discover that many of the human accomplishments that we view as grand are small in comparison to the forces of nature at work on our planet.

8   Pathways to Discovery

This book contains information about all the pathways within or leading into the Monument. Some are roads, some are trails, and others are climbing routes. It provides information that will be valuable to you in discovering Mount St. Helens in every season.

There is a 16 page section of previously unpublished color photos that begins on page 113. Prints of these photos are made available to you at a reasonable cost by use of the ordering instructions on the last page of the book.

Mount St. Helens is a wonderful place to visit. You'll want to come often and discover new evidence of the creative forces at work. Plan to spent a few days or weeks and develop a lasting romance with America's favorite volcano.

Table of Contents

INTRODUCTION

Most first time visitors to Mount St. Helens are surprised at the amount of time it takes to get to the best points of interest. There are significant changes currently taking place in how you can access the area, and you will find in this book the most up-to-date information on how to make the best use of your time while planning a safe, comfortable, and most enjoyable trip to this exciting place.

How to use this Visitor Guide

This guide is organized to make your trip planning easy. Key areas are presented in individual chapters. Information on suitability for children, access for the disabled, open season, special clothing, and other specific needs are presented in these individual chapters. Later in this introduction there is general information on the climate and preparing for the trip as well as information on roads and trails. A travel distance summary chart will help you determine how much time to allow for driving to the principle attractions from the nearby major population centers. More specific information on history and geology is presented in the specific chapters on individual features.

If you already have an idea about where you think you want to go, you can turn to that section by going to the Table of Contents or Index and finding the appropriate page number. For example, if you want to climb the mountain or find a trail for horse riding in old growth on your next trip, check the index and turn to those pages.

Spectacular views await you on the many new pathways around Mount St. Helens. This view from Norway Pass on Boundary Trail No. 1 is your reward for a 2.2 miles hike.

Recommendations on where to go

First time visitors: Plan to visit the Mount St. Helens Visitor Center at Silver Lake, five miles east of Castle Rock. The orientation on geology and what happened here on May 18, 1980 will make your trip more meaningful. If you have more than 3 hours remaining after touring the center continue east on SR 504 to the Coldwater Ridge Visitor Center. You'll get the best views of the crater, lava dome, and debris avalanche from here. This is the most exciting place to visit on the Monument and you'll want to return again when the facilities at Johnston Ridge are completed.

Repeat visitors and those able to spend several days: Your choice will depend on time available and personal interest. If you have a full day, (10 to 12 hours), plan to visit Road 99/Spirit Lake area and include the 1.1 mile hike to Spirit Lake on the Harmony Falls Trail. Here you'll get the best views of Spirit Lake and the timber blown down by the lateral blast.

If you are near Woodland, WA on I-5 and have 6 to 8 hours available, visit the lava and mudflow area discussed in Chapter 4. Include Ape Cave Interpretive Site, Trail of Two Forests Interpretive Trail, and Lava Canyon Trail along your route.

If the weather's favorable and you're comfortable in a small aircraft, take either a helicopter or small airplane flight over the area. For as little as $50.00 per person you'll receive a totally different perspective of the May 18, 1980 event.

Most scenic visit: If you can commit 12 hours and are physically able to hike 20 miles in a day, I highly recommend the following hike. Camp in or near Iron Creek Campground, and hike the Boundary Trail No. 1 from Norway Pass Trailhead east across Mt. Margaret Ridge to the rock arch above St. Helens Lake. From this ridge you'll enjoy the classic views of Mount St. Helens which include the crater and lava dome with Spirit Lake in the foreground.

Ultimate visit: If you can commit two days and are in good physical condition, you may want to climb the mountain and view the Monument from this perspective. Read Chapter 5 and get your doctor's opinion before applying for the permit.

Getting around in the Monument

Roads

Driving conditions in the Monument are a lot different than on the interstate and state highways. The two lane asphalt surfaced roads will resemble the state highways, but must be driven at slower speeds because of curves and lack of guard rails. Some of the roads are single lane and have gravel surfaces. You need to be very careful on these roads to use the turnouts and stay to the right in the extra width provided around curves to allow oncoming traffic to pass.

Dust will be a problem most of the summer season and driving with your lights on is suggested. Fill your windshield wiper fluid container before leaving home as a dirty windshield could cause an accident.

Leave your trailer at the campground or one of the suggested drop-off locations provided.

Trails

Type of use

There is no motorized use allowed on trails within the legislated Monument except with a permit, and these are limited to research and administration. The use of mountain bikes, horses, and llamas is restricted on some trails. Generally this is limited to the area impacted by the May 18, 1980 blast, and the more heavily used or interpretive trails. This guide presents information on types of use permitted. This information could change, and you should check with the Monument Headquarters if you have any concerns about a particular trail. Each trail should be signed at the trailhead or point of entry with information regarding use permitted or restricted.

A user friendly computerized trail information system, TRIS, is available at all Recreation Equipment Incorporated (REI) stores, and other locations. This information should be current.

Trailhead signing at the Monument is excellent.

Safety

Never go exploring off the roads alone. If something happens to you, you will need someone to go for help. Always be prepared to spend the night. Carry the following ten essentials:

1.   Matches in a water proof container
2.   Extra clothing
3.   Extra food
4.   Sunglasses
5.   Knife
6.   Candle or other heat source for starting a fire with wet wood
7.   First aid kit
8.   Flashlight
9.   Map
10.   Compass

If you climb the mountain or go cross-country hiking, travel in a group of at least four. If someone goes down with a leg injury or worse yet a stroke, one person can stay with the injured while two go for help.

Difficulty level

One piece of trail information that you'll see used in this book, on maps, and on TRIS to describe trails is the difficulty level. This information will help you decide which trail matches your own personal physical condition and skill level. This is new terminology that will be applied to describe all trails across the country. There are three difficulty levels: easy, more difficult, and most difficult.

Easiest   Requires limited skill and has little physical challenge. Tread is smooth, level, and wide with generous clearing of trees, limbs, and other vegetation above and to each side of the trail to permit easy passage. Elevation gain or loss is minimal. Streams are most often crossed by bridges. Suitable for children and anyone looking for a leisure walk.

More
difficult

Requires a moderate skill level and provides a moderate physical challenge. Tread surface contains roots and embedded rocks. Clearing of trees, limbs, and other vegetation above and to each side of the trail results in occasional inconvenience to the users. Elevation gain or loss may be as much as 1500 feet per mile. Streams are sometimes crossed by fords. Suitable for those in normal physical condition.

Most
Difficult

Requires a high degree of skill and provides a lot of physical challenge. Tread is seldom graded except on steep side slopes for safety and prevention of soil erosion. Minimal clearing of trees, limbs, and other vegetation results in hampering your progress. Elevation gain or loss can be sever, 2000 feet per mile. Streams are crossed by fording and they're sometimes difficult. Suitable for experienced users in good physical condition.

The difficulty level will directly affect how much distance you can travel per hour. It will probably take twice as long to go a mile on a most difficult trail than on an easy trail. You'll find that walking on an easy trail is much slower than on a sidewalk. Figure about 2 mph for older children and adults. Add 15 minutes per mile for every 500 feet of vertical rise. If you're a beginner or have small children double your estimate of time, or put your faith in the time estimates presented in this book.

Pets

Although taking your pets for a walk in the forest may seem like the right thing to do, I recommend that you leave them at home. Even a well-behaved dog can ruin someone else's trip. Dogs often bark to defend a territory or to guard their master. They also defecate in the middle of the trail. Even though some dogs do not chase wildlife, their very presence is sensed by many small wild animals as a threat. Some trails are closed to pets. You should check before bringing a pet to the Monument.

Horses

Most horse riders and llama users do their best to be good neighbors on the trail. When a hiker or mountain biker meets someone with one of these animals, the rule is that the animals have the right of way. The hiker should get off the trail, preferably, on the downhill side. Continue normal motion and speak to the animals so that the animals recognize you as another human, and you don't suddenly surprise them. An out of control mountain bike is the biggest threat to everyone. If you're on a mountain bike you should travel at a safe speed and dismount and yield to the animals, and hikers.

The area around Spirit Lake and the backcountry to the north was one of the most popular horse riding areas in the state until the eruption. Now, because of the high value placed on studying the natural processes, horse use is restricted from most of the area impacted by the lateral blast. It's mostly because these animals can bring in exotic plant seeds that would be deposited when they defecate. This would have a very noticeable effect on the new plant community. The Forest Service has provided many new trail opportunities to replace those lost in the blast area.

Maps

Most of the trails discussed in the text are described sufficiently to get around safely with the Mount St. Helens National Volcanic Monument Map available at the information stations and visitor centers. Some backpackers wanting to leave the trail or plan long overnight hikes may want to purchase contour maps of the area. If you need this much detail, check on the following USGS Quad maps. The appropriate quad map is indicated at the beginning of each section that includes descriptions of trails. Most of the maps available from private retailers do not have the newest trails shown. The Monument Headquarters will sell these maps with the most up-to-date information.

Quad No.	Quad Name
D17.1	Vanson Peak
D17.2	Cowlitz Falls
D18.1	Greenhorn Buttes
D16.4	Elk Rock
D17.3	Spirit Lake West
D17.4	Spirit Lake East
D18.3	French Butte

E16.2	Goat Mt.
E17.1	Mount St. Helens
E17.2	Smith Creek Butte
E18.1	Spencer Butte
E17.3	Mt. Mitchell
E17.4	Cedar Flats
E18.3	Burnt Peak
E18.2	Quartz Creek Butte

The maps in the appendix of this book show the trail numbers and segments that are described in the text. These trail segments are not signed on the ground, but are used on these maps to help you to locate portions of the longer trails.

Accessibility

Whenever it was possible, new facilities in the Monument were constructed so they may be accessed by everyone. All of the information stations, viewpoints, and toilets are barrier-free, and some of the trails provide several difficulty levels that are barrier-free. Throughout the book this information on accessibility will be surrounded by a border so it is easy to locate.

Other safety

Reporting Emergencies

There are several emergency telephones located around the Monument so that you can request help. These phones are in most instances solar operated, an interesting technology.

Forest Services employees can be flagged down and asked for assistance.

The North Country Emergency Medical Service is on patrol in the area during most of the heavy use season, and has an ambulance stationed at the

Pine Creek Information Station. There will be a similar emergency medical service provided on the west side at or near the eastern end of SR 504.

Volcanic Risk

The volcano is in a period of quiet. The Geological Survey believes that it can predict any eruptions in sufficient time to give visitors enough advanced notice to move to safety. Avoid going into areas that are closed, like the crater, and you'll be ok.

Water

The water is not safe to drink. Drinking water opportunities are limited throughout most of the Monument. If it comes out of a pipe or pump, it's probably safe. One exception is the Kalama Horse Camp where the piped water is only approved for the livestock. Nearby, Kalama Springs is probably pure as it flows out of the earth, but no one is testing it. Also, Short Creek on the Loowit Trail just above June Lake flows out of the lava and is the only natural water on that entire 26 miles of trail. It's best to bring lots of drinking water with you.

Theft

You would think that there would be few thieves in a national park or monument. Unfortunately, your chance of getting your car or camp broken into is higher here than at home. The greatest risk occurs at trailheads that are off the main road. The best advise is to avoid leaving anything in the car that you can't afford to loose. If you do leave valuables behind when you go on one of the trails, do not leave them where they can be seen. Avoid parking a car or pickup truck in seldom visited trailheads, especially if the vehicle has mag-wheels, compact disk or other stereo player that is visible.

Protecting the Land

Every visitor to the Monument should be a collector of litter and garbage. Please notice that there are no garbage cans. The increasing cost of collecting and hauling garbage was to the point of taking most of the budget, and years ago the decision was made to ask the visitors to help by packing their litter and garbage out. Most people are happy to do this because it allows for other services, such as an interpreter to be available. Please join in and help by picking up any litter that you see. Avoid the temptation to dispose of garbage in the toilets as it increases the Forest Service cost for pumping these vaults.

You should not become a collector of rocks, plants, and artifacts. The Monument was created to protect the natural features and processes, and it is illegal to remove these items. It seems like there's an endless supply of pumice here, but good samples to look at in the area around viewpoints are becoming increasingly more difficult to find. Visitors have been scooping them up to take home. The ones left behind are being trampled into fine powder and blown away by the wind. As the next several decades pass there will be less and less evidence of the eruption for visitors to examine. Please help by resisting the temptation to take home samples.

The new pumice is very fragile and will crumble under foot. You can prevent most damage to the resource by staying in the area that has been developed for you. Please stay on the trails, stay behind the rock walls, use the stairways provided, and don't walk on or pick the new vegetation.

Climate and being prepared

Summer/Fall

When most people think about the Northwest they think about rain. Although it is true that it rains a lot, especially in the Cascade Mountains where the clouds blowing in from the Pacific rise and cool causing rain, the area is blessed with the most beautiful summer weather in the nation. Usually the rain stops in middle to late June and it's beautiful clear sunny weather until late in October. The weather can change very quickly from this sunny condition so be prepared for sudden drops in temperature and the possibility of rain.

Interpretive signing allows exciting visits even during storms.

The daily temperature change is dramatic. You can count on a temperature drop as soon as the sun sets. In July and August you may have high temperatures in the 80 to 90 degree Fahrenheit range , and drop to the 50 degree range during the night. The message here is to be prepared. Always carry extra clothing, especially if you leave the road.

A sudden change in the weather from sunny to rainy will also result in a similar drop in temperature. Getting wet and cold can be very uncomfortable and result in catching cold or developing hypothermia. When leaving your car for an extended length of time, such as to ride or hike a trail, take a day pack with extra clothing. Many locals dress in layers so that they can add or subtract items of clothing during the day. Wool and gortex seem to be the favored materials.

 Many of the places that you'll be directed to will be in the blast area. The forest that once covered this large area was either buried by the landslide, blown away or toppled-over by the lateral blast during the May 18th, 1980 eruption. As a result there is no shade for miles in all directions. At this elevation the summer sun will burn exposed skin, and can have harmful effects on the eyes. You should be prepared with sunscreen (14 or higher), sunglasses, and a hat. It is somewhat like a desert environment. If you plan to go on the trails, bring about one quart of water per person per each three hours on the trail.

Winter

Snow starts falling on the area around November 1st. The exception is on the area of Mount St. Helens above timberline where snow storms could occur at anytime. The east side access is normally obstructed by snow by the end of November. The visitor centers at Silver Lake and Coldwater Ridge are open all year.

Some years there is enough snow at the two Snoparks to begin cross-country skiing and snowmobiling during the Christmas Holidays. The snow is very wet and heavy, and normally will accumulate to about 6 feet deep at the Snopark areas. Snow depth at Elk Pass on Road 25 and on Road 99 will exceed 10 feet in most years and will block access to the eastside of the Monument until Memorial Day.

Daytime temperatures will usually be in the 30's, and drop to below freezing during the night. Most winters there are several cold periods scattered throughout December through February. These cold snaps only last for a couple of weeks. It's usually clear, and temperatures will drop to the low teens. This is usually followed by longer periods of warmer temperatures and rain. This freezing and thawing creates very favorable conditions for avalanches. Mount St. Helens and especially the area around the Plains of Abraham is well known for avalanche hazard.

If you travel into the area after October 1, it's a good idea to carry traction devices. Bring along some extra dry clothing so that you can change when you get wet. Always fill up your gas tank before heading into the Monument and make sure someone knows where you're going. Take along some food, trail mix, and hot beverage.

Spring

The winter recreation season usually lasts until April 1st. Some of the early spring attractions are Ape Cave and the Trail of Two Forests on the south side of the mountain, the waterfalls on the North Fork of the Lewis River, and the big trees at Quartz Cr. and Iron Cr. south of Randle. Except for the visitor centers at Silver Lake and Coldwater Ridge, information services and maintenance are at a reduced level until after Memorial Day.

Mount St. Helens Trivia

There are occasional bits of triva about Mount St. Helens presented throughout this book at the end of some chapters such as:

In 1908 the lands roughly bounded by the Columbia River, Mount St. Helens, Mount Adams and Mount Rainier National Park were incorporated into the Columbia National Forest. This Forest was renamed in 1949, the Gifford Pinchot National Forest in honor of the first chief of the Forest Service.

On August 27, 1982 President Reagan signed into law an Act setting aside 110,000 acres around the volcano as the Mount St. Helens National Volcanic Monument, the Nation's first such Monument. At that time it was the third National Monument managed by the Forest Service. Admiralty Island and Misty Fjord National Monuments in Alaska were the other two.

Chapter 1   Information and Orientation

Visitor Centers

Mount St. Helens Visitor Center at Silver Lake

From Exit 49, Castle Rock, on Interstate 5
5 miles east on SR 504
Allow a minimum of 1 hour
Open daily 9 a.m. to 6 p.m., mid-April to mid-Sept and 9 a.m. to 5 p.m.
the rest of the year.
Closed Thanksgiving, Christmas and other winter holidays.
Ideal for children.

This is the best place to go to start your adventure into the Mount St. Helens National Volcanic Monument. A well-informed friendly staff will help you plan your trip. There are two audiovisual programs in the theater that will increase your understanding of the recent eruptions of this most active volcano in the lower 48 states, and make your trip a more memorable experience. The programs are: **"This Place in Time"**, a 22 minute movie about the past, the 1980 eruptions, and the future, and **"Mount St. Helens"**, a 10 minute slide program that uses 15 projectors to help you relive the 1980 eruption. These award winning programs are alternated every half hour, and it's worth the time to see both of them.

When you exit the theater you'll be headed into the display area. You'll be able to compare Mount St. Helens with other volcanoes and learn what scientists believe causes volcanoes. You'll learn about the people that used thearea and how they responded to the eruptions. There's a large walk-through model of Mount St. Helens that allows you to see a magma chamber inside the volcano. There is information on the monitoring of the

A friendly and helpful staff greet over 600,000 visitors each year at the visitor center at Silver Lake.

current activity by the Geological Survey, and some equipment provided for you to acquire a hands-on experience.

This award winning building is totally accessible. The outside trails are also barrier-free and the free telescopes for viewing Mount St. Helens are placed appropriately for use by someone seated in a wheel chair. The movie is in closed captions, and brochures are available in large print and foreign languages. Hearing assistance devices are available for theater programs.

The Visitor Center is set in Seaquest State Park on the shoreline of Silver Lake. The State of Washington has a 70 unit campground here, and it is the best possible camping opportunity if you're going to visit the west side of the Monument. It's a short walk between the campground and visitor center and a tunnel allows visitors to walk underneath SR 504. Additional information on this campground is included in chapter 10.

Silver Lake was formed by mudflows from Mount St. Helens about 2500 to 3000 years ago. The shallow 3500 acre lake provides good habitat for bass, and is considered to be the best bass fishing opportunity in Southwest Washington. It also provides hundreds of acres of marsh for waterfowl and is a prime bird watching area.

Woodcarvings: Take time to examine the handtooled woodcarvings on the massive columns of western red cedar that support this unique building. These carvings on panels of western big leaf maple mounted on the columns are reminiscent of the fine craftsmanship of an earlier time in our history. The 16 murals depict northwest landscapes from ancient valley forest to high mountain country. The various plants and animals designed into them form a theme of emerging life. It took Joe Valasek and his assistant, Kim Lewis, seven months to complete the carvings.

The murals nearest the entrance illustrate the Pacific silver fir zone. Those in the central lobby depict lowland valley forests which contain western red cedar, Douglas-fir, western hemlock and vine maple. The panels nearest the theater show the higher elevation sub-alpine zone with Roosevelt elk and mountain goats roaming among mountain hemlock, sub-alpine fir and white bark pine.

Mannequins: In the display area the ash-gray mannequins depict the diversity of people that played important roles in the human history of the Spirit Lake area. They represent a fur trapper, (1811-1835), an Indian berry picker, (1870-1910), a miner, (1890-1912), a summit climber, (1960-1980), and a forest service ranger, (1908-1980).

Everyone who lives in, or visits, the Northwest should spend a little time at this visitor center. It's an important part of your visit to the volcano and will give you the background information that will make your trip most enjoyable. It's conveniently located for going west on SR 504 to the best view points of the crater and lava dome. It's also handy if you're traveling along I-5. Once you discover it you'll want to return often with friends and out-of-town visitors.

There's a good selection of educational materials such as books, brochures, maps, and pictures for sale at the center.

Special programs are sometimes available for groups. For additional information phone (206) 274-6644 or 274-4038 for a recording.

Mount St. Helens Visitor Center at Kelso

> **I-5, exit 39, Kelso**
> **East side of the freeway at the exit**
> **Allow a minimum of 30 minutes**
> **Open daily all year**

This visitor center operated by the Kelso Chamber of Commerce provides interpretation of the May 18, 1980 mudflow in the Toutle and Cowlitz rivers. The scale model of Mount St. Helens and these rivers gives a different perspective of the event, and helps orient you to the rivers and the threat that they posed to the Kelso/Longview communities.

There is also a memorial to the 57 people who lost their lives as a result of the 1980 eruption.

> *Although the building, a double wide trailer, is barrier-free the access ramp is steep and the passage ways between displays are narrow. Those in wheelchairs may need a little help.*

A well-informed staff is available to help you plan your journey into the area. Some books and maps are for sale. For more information call (206) 577-8058.

Coldwater Ridge Visitor Center

> **SR 504 about 44 miles east of Castle Rock**
> **Open daily all year, 9 a.m. to 6 p.m., mid-April to mid-Sept. and 9 a.m.**
> **to 5 p. m. the rest of the year.**
> **Closed Thanksgiving, Christmas, and other winter holidays.**

There is interpretation and the latest information on the volcano, research, and places to go at this visitor center. It provides the best view of the crater and lava dome and is discussed in detail in Chapter 2.

Information Stations

When the area around Mount St. Helens was reopened to visitors in 1982, many of the roads were damaged and hazards from the volcano were high. Information stations were established along the principle routes into the area so that visitors could be warned of road conditions and volcano behavior. Over the years these information stations have been improved and are still providing up-to-date information on road conditions and help visitors find the best location for their planned activities.

Woods Creek Information Station

Forest Service Road 25
About 6 miles south of Randle
Open daily, May to October, 9 a.m. to 5 p.m.

This is a convenient place to pick up information on your way to Road 99 and the Spirit Lake viewpoints. You can either have your questions answered at a drive-up window without leaving your car or go inside and visit with an interpreter. There are interesting displays and books, brochures, maps and slides for sale. The Woods Creek Watchable Wildlife Area is across the road and provides picnic tables, drinking water, and additional restrooms. After a long ride in the car this is a good place to take a short walk on the barrier-free trail around the beaver pond.

Barrier-free compost type toilets, picnic tables and trail are available.

Pine Creek Information Station

Forest Service Road 90
About 20 miles east of Cougar
Open daily, 9 a.m. to 6 p. m., May 1 to Sept. 30

This is the former ranger station for the St. Helens Ranger District at the time of the 1980 eruption. On March 27, 1980, one week after the earth began to quake, a loud explosion that sounded like a sonic boom was heard at this site signaling the reawakening of Mount St. Helens and the immediate evacuation of this office and living quarters. The ranger district was operated out of trailers provided by the Federal Emergency Management Agency, FEMA, in Cougar until May 18th when the main eruption forced it's closure.

This is a convenient location to pick up information on your way from Woodland to Road 99 or the Lewis River area. A well-informed staff will help you with travel directions to points of interest. There are interesting displays of places to visit on the south side of the mountain. The movie "This Place in Time" is shown continuously on video tape. You can buy maps, books, etc..

Drinking water and an emergency telephone are available. It's possible that the North Country Emergency Service ambulance will be nearby.

The display area and rest rooms are barrier free.

Ape's Headquarters

Forest Service Road 8303
About 11 miles from Cougar
Open May 1 to Sept. 30, 10 a.m. to 6 p.m.

You won't find any apes working here, but the entrance to Ape Cave, discussed in chapter 4, is only about 100 feet away. If you're going to the cave or any of the attractions on the south and west slopes of the mountain, this is the place to stop and get the latest information.

In addition to the sale of the usual line of books, maps, etc., there are lanterns for rent. For $3.00 plus your drivers license for collateral, you can have the use of a propane lantern, plus a flashlight during your visit to the cave.

The information building, vault toilets, and trail to the cave entrance and information display in a kiosk are barrier-free.

Mount St. Helens National Volcanic Monument Headquarters

SR 503, 3 miles north of Amboy
Open all year, Mon. to Fri., 7:30 a.m. to 5:00 p.m.

If you're approaching the Monument from the south on SR 503, you can stop at the administrative headquarters for information. This is one of the best places to get information after Sept. 30 when the other information stations have closed for the season. It's also the place to get permits and the most up-to-date information on road conditions.

Someday in the future, a new office will be constructed at this location.

Although alterations have been made on the old office building to make it barrier-free, it is difficult access. The visitor area in the information office is very small for someone in a wheelchair. The toilet facility was remodeled to allow wheelchair access.

For more information call (206) 247-5473, or write to Monument Manager, Mount St. Helens National Volcanic Monument, 42218 NE Yale Bridge Road, Amboy, WA 98601.

Randle Ranger Station

U S 12 at Randle, WA
Open all year, Mon. to Fri., 7:45 a.m. to 4:30 p.m.

If you're going through Randle and need information on Mount St. Helens, it's available at the ranger station year round. A good selection of maps, books, videos, etc. are available for sale. The knowledgeable and friendly staff will help you find a campground or suitable trail experience.

For additional information call (206) 497-7565 or write to District Ranger, Randle Ranger Station, Randle, WA 98377.

Gifford Pinchot National Forest Headquarters

> **E. 4 th Plain Blvd. & Andresen, Vancouver**
> **Open all year, Mon. to Fri., 8:00 a.m. to 4:30 p.m.**

If you live in the Portland/Vancouver area, call the Forest Headquarters for information. You can purchase maps here and acquire up-to-date information on roads and trails.

> *The building is barrier-free.*

Call (206) 750-7500 or write to Gifford Pinchot National Forest, 6926 E. 4 th Plain Blvd., P.O. Box 8944, Vancouver, WA 98668-8944.

Mount St. Helens Trivia

The Forest Service opened two temporary visitor centers along Interstate 5 within six weeks after the May 18, 1980 eruption. One was located at exit 14 near Ridgefield and the other in the Lewis and Clark State Park near exit 68. Almost a million visitors were greeted at these centers during the first season of operation.

Chapter 2

Coldwater Ridge Visitor Center & State Route 504

Coldwater Ridge Visitor Center

SR 504, Spirit Lake Memorial Highway
44 miles east of Castle Rock
Allow at least two hours for the round trip from I-5
Allow a minimum of one hour on site
Open daily all year, 9 a.m. to 6 p.m., mid-April to mid-Sept., and 9 a.m. to 5 p.m. the rest of the year
Closed Thanksgiving, Christmas, and other winter holidays

This is the best view of the crater and new lava dome that is accessible by road, and is the most highly recommended attraction for first time visitors. You also can view Coldwater Lake, a new 1050 acre lake created by the giant landslide that slid off the north side of Mount St. Helens on May 18, 1980. In the distance you'll also see a portion of Castle Lake, another 72 acre lake created by that same landslide. Scientists call this landslide, the largest ever recorded by humans, the debris avalanche.

The visitor center building is laid out like a big eagle. On the right, as you enter, is the conservation education wing, and to the left is a concession-operated restaurant, gift shop and book store. An information counter is between the two wings. It has a well-informed and friendly staff that will help you to determine where to go and provide you with information for a better understanding of the volcano.

Coldwater Lake VisitorCenter currently provides the best views of Mount St. Helens accessible by road.

The interpretive displays portray how plant and animal life survived the eruption and illustrate recolonization of the volcanic landscape. An interactive video program "Fire and Life" helps you plan your adventure into the Monument. There is a small theater with a 6 1/2 minute program, "Change of Scenes", shown on a screen made up of 16 video monitors, four monitors high and four wide.

All of the facilities are barrier-free. Messages in the display area are translated into French, German, Spanish, and Japanese and transmitted to individual head sets provided. Programs are also closed captions.

The theme of the display area is "Power of the Eruption & the Resilience of Life". There is a landscape mural covering three walls depicting this theme.

Outside the visitor center is an environmental education trail, **"Winds of Change Trail"**. This short loop trail allows you to become involved with the environment. The center of the loop is the Scientific Training Operation

Program, **STOP**. This area contains 30 succession plots maintained by the Forest Service for study by school groups.

Coldwater Lake

Prior to the May 18, 1980 eruption the area now covered by this lake was forested. The debris avalanche slammed into Coldwater Ridge and formed a natural dam creating a new lake. As the water trapped behind this natural barrier rose, hydrologists became concerned that the unconsolidated material would collapse causing flooding in down stream communities. The U S Army Corp of Engineers was called in to stabilize the dam and reduce the threat.

The Scientific Advisory Board, a group of nationally known scientists set up to monitor the protection of research opportunities, agreed that this lake could be stocked with fish and used for more traditional recreation. Spirit Lake and many of the nearby backcountry lakes, on the other hand, would be left unstocked so scientists will be able to study the natural processes.

Coldwater Lake because of it's shallow depth and abundant feed is capable of producing good size fish in a short time. Thirty thousand Rainbow Trout were first introduced in 1989. The Department of Game anticipates that fish taken will average one and a half pounds. The season opens in late May and closes in Oct.. The first year, 1993, this will be later, perhaps in July, because of construction of the facilities at the boat launch. During this time access to the lake will be by the Elk Branch Trail No. 211D that starts at the visitor center.

The following selective regulations apply: You must use artificial lures with a barbless single-pointed hook, and are limited to one fish that is at least 14 inches in length. You should check with the Washington State Fishing Regulations for the current year for more information.

A boat ramp and picnic area are located near the dam. Boat motors are limited to electric to prevent petroleum products from contaminating the lake and interfering with the natural processes. This also reduces the noise from the boating activity.

Trails

Birth of the Lake Interpretive Trail

> **At the Coldwater Lake Boat Launch**
> **Barrier-free loop, 800 ft.**
> **Hikers only**
> **Allow 30 minutes**

This trail, which will be available in 1994, consists of a boardwalk along the shore of Coldwater Lake. Interpretive signs explain how the May 18, 1980 eruption formed the lake.

Crater Rocks Interpretive Trail No. 229

> **0.3 mile east of the visitor center**
> **Barrier-free loop, 0.2 mile**
> **More difficult loop, 2.2 miles**
> **Hikers only**
> **Allow 30 minutes to one hour**

It's mind expanding to observe that the landscape that you're walking on was so very recently inside Mount St. Helens. This interpretive trail that is divided into a short barrier-free loop, 0.2 mile, and a longer, 2.2 miles, hiking loop explains the debris avalanche and some of the colorful material. The longer loop takes you by several of the newly created small ponds and to the North Fork of the Toutle River. This trail is under construction in 1993 and will be available soon.

Small ponds created by the debris avalanche are emerald green with algae and other new plant life making this a wonderful setting to discover.

Boundary Trail No. 1.1, (Coldwater Lake to Johnston Ridge Observatory)

> **Begins 2.5 miles east of the visitor center**
> **The trailhead at the toe of Johnston Ridge on SR 504 may be under construction.**
> **More difficult, 3.3 miles**
> **Hikers only**
> **Allow 4 hours**

This is the west end of a National Recreation Trail that extends all the way to Counsel Lake at Mount Adams, (56 miles). Someday soon it will be extended to connect with the Pacific Crest National Scenic Trail near the Mount Adams Wilderness. This first section of the trail allows you to hike between the proposed observatory on Johnston Ridge and Coldwater Lake, (3.3 miles), an area impacted by the debris avalanche and the lateral blast. Until the state highway is extended to Johnston Ridge, this is the best way to gain access to the better views of the crater and dome. The trail is more difficult with an elevation gain of 1800 feet. The road access to the trailhead may be blocked because of construction of the highway to Johnston Ridge. You'll need to check at the information counter at the visitor center before planning to use this trail.

Lakes Trail No. 211, (Boat Launch to Trail No. 230)

> **Begins at Coldwater Lake Boat Launch or take Spur Trail No. 211D at the Coldwater Ridge Visitor Center.**
> **More difficult, small elevation gain, 5.3 miles**
> **Hikers only**
> **Allow 4 hours round trip**

This trail follows along the north shoreline of Coldwater Lake and someday should extend through the Mt. Margaret Backcountry and tie into the Boundary Trail No. 1 near Bear Pass. This segment, scheduled for completion in 1993, is 5.3 miles long and ends at the Coldwater Trail No. 230. It will provide good foot access for fishing and sight seeing. It is accessed from either the boat ramp or from the visitor center. Use **Elk Branch Trail No. 211D** when parked at the visitor center. This 3/4 mile tie between the visitor center and Trail No. 211 has a change in elevation of 600 feet.

Coldwater Trail No. 230, (Trail No. 211 to Trail No. 1)

> **Starts at Trail No. 211 at upper end of the lake**
> **More difficult, 2500 ft. elevation gain, 4.5 miles**
> **Hikers only**
> **Allow about 6 hours round trip**

This trail climbs for 4.5 miles and ties into the Boundary Trail No. 1 near St. Helens Lake. It's just a short distance down Trail No. 1 to one of the most interesting sights. The Boundary Trail goes through a natural rock arch. As you go through one way you look at Mount

St. Helens, and if you turn around you can see Mount Adams. It's a difficult hike when added to the 5.3 miles of Trail No. 211. On the return you can take Trail No. 230A for variety, and a shorter 2.5 miles to Coldwater Lake. It's best to leave your vehicle at the boat ramp. The trail takes you by some of the logging equipment that was destroyed by the eruption.

You also can look into a portion of the backcountry and see the effect of the lateral blast on that very rugged terrain.

So. Coldwater Trail No. 230A, (Coldwater Lake to Trail No. 230)

Leaves SR 504 1.2 miles beyond the boat launch
More difficult, 1500 ft. elevation gain, 2.5 miles
Hikers only
Allow 2 hours round trip

This 2.5 mile trail allows visitors to have a close look at some of the logging equipment destroyed in 1980, and provides an alternate loop opportunity in conjunction with Trails No. 211 and No. 230. The lower end will be impacted during the road construction activity in the vicinity of Coldwater Lake.

Johnston Ridge Observatory

The view from Johnston Ridge stuns the senses. How could a spectacle of such awesome power and beauty be within just a couple hours drive of two major U.S. cities. When the debris avalanche roared down the slopes of Mount St. Helens, it slammed into this ridge. The tremendous force of this giant landslide caused a portion of it to slide up and over the ridge, about 1150 feet vertically, and continue into South Coldwater Creek. This is the only place in the world where this type of geologic feature can be observed.

Trail planner locating the Boundary Trail No. 1 on Johnston Ridge near the proposed observatory.

Access

The state highway is being extended for 9 miles from Coldwater Lake to the top of Johnston Ridge. When this road access is completed about 1995 you'll be able to drive to the best viewpoint of the crater and dome. It will be the one place in the Monument that everyone should visit on their first trip. This experience is more awesome than being on the rim of the Grand Canyon or being in the first row of seats to watch Old Faithful.

The original plan was to access this excellent viewpoint using an aerial tram from the parking area at Coldwater Ridge to protect the remains of the deposits of the debris avalanche in South Coldwater Creek. The scientists wanted to observe the natural changes occurring on this material that spilled over the top of Johnston Ridge during the landslide.

Tunnel

This new highway will pass just above the outlet of the tunnel that was used to stabilize the level of Spirit Lake.

As the new Spirit Lake continued to fill up with water from rain and snow melt, scientists began to predict that the natural dam formed by the unconsolidated material in the debris avalanche would washout. It was believed that this would occur when the water overtopped the natural dam, and that the water would be released in one giant flood. This would cause extreme loss of life and property in the areas downstream. It was predicted that water would be about 10 feet deep in downtown Longview.

The President declared a state of emergency and authorized the US Army Corps of Engineers to solve the problem. The final solution would be to drill an 11 foot diameter tunnel for about 8500 feet through Harrys Ridge and drain excess water into South Coldwater Creek. This required that a road be constructed to the tunnel outlet in the upper part of South Coldwater Creek. This road and the additional water diverted into Coldwater Creek from Spirit Lake significantly changed the research potential of the area. The research community and the public recommended that the road be improved and continued to Johnston Ridge. This evolved into the present plan for extending the state highway to the viewpoint.

Observatory

This building will be dug into the top of Johnston Ridge and partially buried to protect the natural appearance of the volcanic landscape. The volcano is 5 miles to the south, but you have the feeling of being right there. You'll experience a breath-taking view that includes the crater, new lava dome, a portion of Spirit Lake, the debris avalanche, and the new pumice plain between the mountain and the lake. You'll be seated in an outdoor amphitheater and listen to an interpreter explain the dynamics of this volcano.

Inside you'll be able to examine displays on the eruptions of 1980 and the monitoring by scientists from the Geological Survey. An audiovisual program will help you understand this landscape. The informed and friendly staff will help you select an adventure to match your skills and interest.

This building and the immediate area outside will be barrier-free.

Trails

Boundary Trail No. 1, (Observatory to Road 26)

> **Accessed at the observatory or parking area**
> **Barrier-free for the first 300 ft.**
> **More difficult, 14.2 miles**
> **Hikers only to Trail No. 230**
> **Hikers and mountain bikes from Trail No. 230 to Road 26 at Norway Pass Trailhead**

This trail was mentioned in the section on Coldwater Lake, but is mentioned here again because when Johnston Ridge is open to the public, about 1995 or 96, it will become the primary trailhead. You'll want to hike to the east to Harrys Ridge Viewpoint which is the premium view of the Monument. The views of Spirit Lake, Bear Cove, and the lava dome within the crater are excellent.

It's about a 7 mile round trip to Harrys Ridge from the Observatory. The trail is easy to more difficult for hiking. There is no shade and at this elevation the ultraviolet sun rays will quickly burn uncovered skin. Use a good sun screen, wear a hat and sunglasses, and carry drinking water. There will be a shelter and toilets. Allow about 3.5 hours.

This trail will take you through the debris avalanche overtopping of the ridge. It's a desert-like landscape and gives you a Death Valley type experience. If you're in good physical condition continue east on the Boundary Trail, (uphill), for about one more mile to the natural rock arch. It's one of the unique features in the Monument. If you're a backpacker you may wish to continue all the way across Mt. Margaret Ridge to Norway Pass Trailhead on Road 26, (14.2 miles). This takes you by the classic views of Mount St. Helens with Spirit Lake in the foreground. This portion of the Boundary Trail is discussed in more detail in Chapter 6.

This is such a unique and fragile landscape that we could very easily destroy it. Help the Forest Service preserve this important resource by staying on the trail and resisting the temptation to take a small piece home.

At about 2.2 miles east of the Observatory the trail junctions with the Truman Trail No. 207. This trail allows you to hike down through the overtopping material to Spirit Lake, and continue on to Windy Ridge, (7 miles).

Boundary Trail Distances From Observatory

Feature	Miles
East	
Truman Trail No. 207 Jct.	2.2
Harrys Ridge Trail No. 208	3.2
Natural arch on Trail No. 1	4.4
Coldwater Trail No. 230 Jct.	4.6
Cold water Peak Trail No. 1F Jct.	5.2
Norway Pass/Trail No. 227 Jct.	12.0
Norway Pass Trailhead/Road 26	14.2
West	
David Johnston Memorial	0.5
Coldwater Lake Trailhead on SR 504	3.3

State Route 504 Spirit Lake Memorial Highway

When the debris avalanche slammed into Johnston Ridge the bulk of the debris was deflected by the ridge down the North Fork of the Toutle River. It took only about 10 minutes for this debris, consisting of boulders, pebbles, sand, silt, and large blocks of glacial ice to flow 13.5 miles down the valley covering over 24 square miles of the valley bottom to an average depth of 150 feet. Later in the day as the debris began to settle, water began to accumulate at the surface from the blocks of melting glacial ice and from the buried river. This accumulated water soon developed into a massive mudflow that moved down the Toutle River destroying everything in its path on it's way to the Cowlitz and Columbia rivers. Damage by the mudflow has been estimated at over $1.2 billion, including 220 homes damaged or destroyed.

The temperature of the Cowlitz River, 45 miles from the mountain, rose to 90 degrees F. This flooding wiped out roads and homes and deposited about 45 million cubic yards of sediment in the Columbia River blocking the deep water navigation channel about 75 miles from the mountain. The Toutle River Bridge on I-5 was closed to north bound traffic because of the high water.

State Route 504, the principle access to Spirit Lake, was blocked by the loss of all of it's bridges and the total destruction of the eastern 26 miles of road. You can still see evidence of the damage as you drive this Spirit Lake Memorial Highway today.

High Retention Dam

The Corps of Engineers removed much of the original sediment from the rivers and you'll see some of it piled along I-5 between the Toutle River Bridge and Kelso. Sediment continued to rapidly refill the river channels each winter during rain storms. The Corps had themselves a permanent dredging job unless something was done to stop the movement of the material from the debris avalanche. In 1989 the Corps completed construction of a sediment retention structure on the North Fork of the Toutle River. This concrete and earth dam is 184 feet high, and is currently trapping the sediment before it can move downstream and do damage. You can see the dam by taking the road to a viewpoint a few miles east of Kid Valley.

Mount St Helens Tree Farm

Weyerhaeuser Company, which has owned and managed the Mount St. Helens Tree Farm since 1900, was the largest private landowner impacted by the eruption. About 14 %, nearly 68,000 acres of the tree farm, was devastated. The mudflow also washed away 650 miles of roads, 19 bridges and 16 miles of railroad and destroyed logging camps, buildings, and vehicles.

By September of 1980 Weyerhaeuser Company began to salvage log the trees that had been toppled by the blast. Quick action was necessary to avoid loss of the wood to insects and disease. More than 1000 people were involved, and during peak summer periods more than 600 truck loads of logs were removed each day. By November 1982 most of the recovery was completed. About 850 million board feet of timber was saved, enough to build 85,000 three-bedroom houses.

Weyerhaeuser Company has planted about 18.4 million trees in the area salvaged. The trees planted in 1981 have already grown to a height of 25 to 35 feet. You'll drive through large areas along SR 504 that have been reforested. Compare this to the much slower natural recovery around the Coldwater Ridge Visitor Center within the National Monument.

Other SR 504 Sites

Most of the damage along SR 504 has been repaired with the construction of the new highway and the regrowth of alder along the river. You'll be able to experience some of the destruction of the mudflow by stopping at the North Fork Survivor's House near Kid Valley, about 20 miles from Interstate 5. Take time to visit the A-Frame house that was filled with mud from the mudflow. Discover that destruction of property and loss of life can occur long distances from volcanoes because of mudflows racing down rivers.

This area called Maple Flats was the end of the road for many years, as most of the old state highway to the east was destroyed by the mudflow during the eruption. The Forest Service opened a small visitor center in the Washington State Highway Maintenance Shop in 1981 and operated it for two seasons.

Stop at the North Fork Toutle River 19 Mile House and enjoy huckleberry short-cake made from berries picked at Mount St. Helens. Browse the gift shop and strike up a conversation with the salesperson. This is a good way to discover the human side of living next to an active volcano.

Mount St. Helens Trivia

Harrys Ridge was named for Geological Survey geologist Harry Glickan rather than Harry Truman. David Johnston had traded week-end duty on May 18, 1980, with Harry Glickan and died on the ridge which was at that time named Coldwater Ridge. This ridge has been renamed Johnston Ridge. Harry Glickan was killed in 1991 while monitoring an eruption at Mount Unzen in Japan.

Chapter 3

Spirit Lake Viewpoints

Roads 99/25

Until 1993 Road 99 was the best access for viewing the evidence of the recent eruption. The interpretive programs and view at Windy Ridge were attracting several hundred thousand visitors each year. The Forest Service anticipates that many first time visitors will now go to Coldwater Lake because of the shorter driving time required. Visitors will continue to come to Windy Ridge, but as second time visitors with more time to spend, and a desire to be more involved with the changing landscape. It takes about 2.5 hours to drive to Windy Ridge Viewpoint at the end of Road 99 from Interstate 5. This is about the same whether you come from the south through Woodland, or the north via US 12.

We'll start the description of things to do and places to visit along Road 99 and 25 with Windy Ridge Viewpoint because of the importance of that site for learning about the 1980 eruptions. Most visitors will come directly to Windy Ridge Viewpoint with perhaps one quick stop at Bear Meadow to use the toilets. You may wish to plan your visit that way, and stop at the other viewpoints and trails as time permits. The other facilities are described in the order you will encounter them as you return from Windy Ridge. You may also want to stop at Wakapish Sno-Park on Road 99 near the junction with Road 25, and drop off your camping trailer, or stop at Woods Creek Information Station on Road 25 a few miles outside of Randle.

Windy Ridge Viewpoint

Located at the end of Road 99, 37 miles from Randle
Allow 2.5 hours driving time from I-5 (one way)
Allow a minimum of 60 minutes on site
25 minute talks scheduled hourly on the 1/2 hour
Open June 15 to Labor Day

The views of Spirit Lake from this and other viewpoints along Road 99 are the best that you'll achieve from any road. Windy Ridge Viewpoint at the end of Road 99 has been the most popular viewing area until the recent opening of SR 504 and the Coldwater Lake Visitor Center. It's still worth seeing because of the opportunity to view Spirit Lake, and extensive areas impacted by the blast. You'll also have opportunities to take trails closer to the crater and Spirit Lake.

At the amphitheater at Windy Ridge an interpreter describes the geologic forces that changed the surrounding landscape.

Plan your arrival time so that you can listen as an interpreter tells about the incredible power unleashed on May 18, 1980. These talks .are scheduled Mon. to Fri., 11:30 a.m. to 4:30 p. m., and Sat. to Sun., 11:30 a. m. to 5:30 p.m.. The programs usually start in mid-June and continue through Labor Day. The road is usually free of snow about Memorial Day and remains open until snow blocks traffic in November. Interpretive signs provide information if you arrive before or after the interpreters are on site.

You'll see evidence of several phases of the 1980 eruptions.

Debris Avalanche

The view of the debris avalanche is outstanding. Try to imagine what it must have looked like on May 18, 1980 when the entire north side of the mountain suddenly broke loose and slid downhill slamming into Johnston Ridge. Some of the debris avalanche surged over Johnston Ridge, 1200 feet above the valley floor, and continued on down into South Coldwater Creek.

Another portion of the avalanche splashed into Spirit Lake causing the water to rise nearly 200 feet. Water from the lake surged 400 feet or more up the surrounding ridges and washed soil, trees with their roots attached, and all other vegetation into the lake. Look closely and see how clean the lower half of the slope is on the other side of the lake. The new lake is 2500 acres compared to the former size of 1300 acres.

The bulk of the avalanche was deflected westward down the North Fork Toutle River for 14 miles. The hummocky deposit you see is more than 600 feet deep in some places, and averages about 150 feet deep.

Lateral Blast

The sudden unloading of much of the volcano's north flank abruptly released the pressure pent-up inside the mountain. Within a few seconds after the beginning of the debris avalanche a tremendous ground hugging lateral blast of hot gases, rocks, ash, and chunks of ice were released northward at near-supersonic speed.

Evidence of this lateral blast covers an area north of the crater in an arch of nearly 180 degrees, which measures 23 miles across from east to west, and extends northward for about 18 miles. Within the first 6 miles from the crater almost all life was destroyed. Trees were snapped off near the ground and blown away. Farther away trees were stripped of their branches and toppled. Near the outer edge of the blast trees were seared and left standing. Look for some of these trees along road 99 as you return toward the Monument entrance.

Scientists estimate that the energy of this blast was equivalent to at least a few megatons of TNT and greater than the first atomic bomb. The temperature of the blast was estimated to be about 680 degrees F since it melted plastic and charred wood.

Vertical Ash Eruption

A strong vertically directed explosion began very shortly after the lateral blast. A column of ash rose quickly to an altitude of more than 12 miles and began to take on the characteristic mushroom shape. This ash cloud produced lightning that started hundreds of fires in the surrounding forest. This vertical eruption continued for over 9 hours continuing to pump ash into the giant cloud which was being push eastward by the jet-stream. In less than two hours the ash cloud had turned daytime into darkness in central Washington, and it remained dark through the entire day.

The heavier ash particles dropped to earth closer to the volcano, while the ash falling in Yakima and Spokane was very fine almost like talcum powder. The new popcorn-like pumice that you see on the ground is from the 1980 eruption. It's very erosive and easily moved by water. Please help the Forest Service retain this new landscape for others to see and study. Stay on the trails and resist the temptation to take a sample home.

Pyroclastic Flows

Pyroclastic flows are hot mixtures of volcanic rocks and gases that sweep along close to the ground. They are produced from the fallback and downslope movement of fragments from an eruption column or by the direct frothing over at the vent. They have been clocked at up to 450 miles per hour. The flows on the north slope of Mount St. Helens were estimated at 50 to 100 miles per hour. Two weeks after the eruption, when measurements could be safely made, the deposits ranged in temperature from 570 to 785 degrees F.

When the hot material of the pyroclastic flows encountered water or moist ground, the water flashed explosively to steam. These blasts created large pits as ash and steam shot as much as a mile above the ground. You'll easily recognize these pits as they look like giant bomb craters. These pits are called *phreatic craters* and give a moon-scape appearance to the area around the south shore of Spirit Lake.

The parking area, amphitheater, interpretive signs, and toilets are barrier-free.

Trails Accessed from Windy Ridge Viewpoint

For more map detail use USGS Quads E17.1 and D17.3

Sand Ladder Trail No. 242

Most difficult, about 1000 ft.
Hikers only
Elevation change from 4170 ft. to 4500 ft.

Near the toilet building you'll see the beginning of a short trail that climbs to the top of the ridge. Most people come directly to Windy Ridge from either Randle or Bear Meadow and feel the need to stretch after the long ride. This trail gives you that opportunity, but provides very little improvement to the view. Your time can be used better at other places along Windy Ridge. Invest your time and energy in hiking the Harmony Falls Trail to Spirit Lake or the Boundary Trail to Norway Pass or Mt. Margaret.

You are at 4200 feet elevation at the parking lot, and will climb to 4500 feet in less than 1000 feet. This makes for a very strenuous climb. This unique sand ladder has been provided to protect the slope which was being heavily damaged by visitors desiring to see what is on top of the ridge. There are 368 steps and you'll be surprised how much work it is to climb them at this elevation. If you decide to take this trail, go slowly and give yourself frequent rest stops. Please stay on the trail as new plant life is easily damaged.

Truman Trail No. 207, (Windy Ridge to Trail No. 1)

> **Begin at the west end of parking area**
> **More difficult trail, 7 miles**
> **Hikers and mountain bikes, 2 miles to Trail No. 216E**
> **Hikers only, 5 miles from Trail No. 216E to Trail No. 1**

At the west end of the Windy Ridge parking lot you'll notice that there is a gate across the road. This is the primary trail access to the mountain and Spirit Lake. Truman Trail follows this road for about 2 miles to a small parking area at the edge of a gently sloped area that geologists call the Pumice Plain. You may see 4-wheel drive vehicles on this road even though you're limited to hiking or mountain biking. These vehicles are permitted to provide access for research, one of the primary reasons for the creation of the Monument. The area you are about to enter is one of the most important for study of the recovery of natural vegetation and ecosystems. You are required to stay on the trail to protect research values. The Forest Service doesn't want to fine people, but wants to protect the natural features and processes for research. Please help make their job easier and stay on the trails.

Trail No. 207 continues across the Pumice Plain downhill toward Spirit Lake, as a hiker only trail. You'll be crossing the pyroclastic flow and mudflow material that now covers the debris avalanche. At approximately 5 miles from the Windy Ridge parking area you'll pass near where the Mount St. Helen's Lodge and Harry Truman are believed to be buried about 200 feet deep. The trail continues uphill through the portion of the debris avalanche that ran up and over-topped Johnston Ridge. At the top of the ridge it ties into the Boundary Trail at about 7 miles from the Windy Ridge Parking. It's a trip that takes all day and requires good physical condition. It's recommended for those visitors that are backpackers.

Windy Trail No. 216E, (Trail No. 207 to Trail No. 216)

> **More difficult, 0.9 miles**
> **Hikers only**
> **Elevation change from 4120 ft. to 4320 ft.**

At the small parking area for research vehicles, Trail No. 216E takes off toward the mountain. This 0.9 mile trail provides a link to Loowit Trail No. 216 for hikers going west around the mountain. If you continue on Trail No. 216.8 for 1 1/4 miles you'll find **Loowit Falls Trail No. 216F** to the left. It provides access (less than 1000 feet) to a good viewpoint of Loowit Falls, a 250 foot steaming waterfall that flows out of the crater. This is an outstanding experience for backpackers able to make the 8.7 miles round trip.

Abraham Trail No. 216D, (Trail No. 207 to Trail No. 216)

> **More difficult, 2.0 miles**
> **Hikers and mountain bikes**

About 1.8 miles down the road from Windy Ridge, Abraham Trail No. 216D takes off to the left and follows a ridge for 2.0 miles where it connects with the Loowit Trail No. 216 which goes around the mountain at timberline. This piece of trail is steep and very erosive. Short sections of sand ladders have been provided to reduce impacts. It is open to mountain bikes. You should carry your bikes over the ladders to protect the fragile environment.

Loowit Trail No. 216.6, (Trail No. 216D to Trail No. 234)

> **More difficult, 1.8 miles**
> **Hikers and mountain bikes**
> **Elevation change from 4460 ft. to 4440 ft.**

+You then can follow Trail No. 216.6 to the south across the Plains of Abraham for about 1.8 miles to Ape Canyon. If you want to hike to Ape Canyon, it's best to leave a car at the Ape Canyon Trailhead on Road 83, and combine 1.8 miles of Trail No. 207, 2.0 miles of Trail No. 216D, 1.8 miles of Trail No. 216.6, and 5.5 miles of Trail

No. 234 for a very scenic 11.1 mile experience. It is a more difficult hike, and going from Windy Ridge Viewpoint to Ape Canyon is recommended.

This is a favorite for experienced mountain bikers.

Remember that there is no water and no shade on any of these trails. Be prepared with a hat, sun screen, and lots of water.

Loowit Trail No. 216.7, (Trail No. 216D to Trail No. 216E)

> **More difficult, 2.0 miles**
> **Hikers only**
> **Elevation change from 4320 ft. to 4885 ft.**

This segment of the Loowit Trail can be used with the Abraham Trail No. 216D, Windy Trail No. 216E, and Loowit Trail No. 216.8 to make a loop hike to view the Loowit Falls flowing out of the crater. Hikers traveling between Windy Ridge Viewpoint and Road 83 can take a short side trip for about 1 mile to Windy Pass for an outstanding view of the Spirit Lake Basin.

Smith Creek Viewpoint

> **About 1 mile east on Road 99 from Windy Ridge**
> **Picnic tables and toilets**
> **Interpretive signs**

You'll overlook the Smith Creek and Muddy River mudflows, and heavy ashfall areas. There's a different view of Mount St. Helens with a mullet-colored landscape that was uncovered by the mudflow that ran over the Plains of Abraham into Smith Creek. A good place to eat lunch.

Smith Creek Trail No. 225, (Road 99 to Road 8322)

Trailhead is about 1/4 mile east of Smith Creek Viewpoint
Most difficult, 9 miles
Hikers and mountain bikes
Elevation change from 4200 ft. to 1580 ft.

You'll want to hike this trail downhill to Road 8322. It goes through the deepest ashfall from the 1980 eruption, and is a very fragile environment. The trail has a large elevation change in the first 3 miles, about 2400 feet. You'll have to ford the West Fork of Smith Creek and the main creek. Early in the season the water may be waist deep because of snow melt. Late in the day the water is deeper due to increasing snow melt. The best strategy is to leave a vehicle at the trailhead at the end of Road 8322. Recommended for experienced backpackers.

Viewpoints along Road 99 provide panoramic vistas of Spirit Lake.

Donneybrook Viewpoint

2 miles northeast of Windy Ridge
Panaramic view of Spirit Lake
Interpretive signs

Named for a small boat-in campground that was on the shoreline of the previous lake directly below here. You'll get one of the best views of Spirit Lake, and learn about the floating log mat. If you look closely at the waterline on Harrys Ridge, you can see the entrance to the tunnel constructed by the Army Corps of Engineers to control the lake level. The log mat moves around depending on the wind direction. Many of the floating logs are over five feet in diameter. How long do you think they'll continue to float? My guess is another 50 years.

Cedar Creek Viewpoint

3 miles east of Windy Ridge Viewpoint
View of Spirit Lake

Another good view of Spirit Lake and a chance to reflect on a Native American point of view on Spirits. The viewpoint was named for the small boat-in campground that is buried beneath the lake directly below here.

Harmony Falls Viewpoint

3.5 miles east of Windy Ridge Viewpoint
View of Spirit Lake

Enjoy my favorite viewpoint and interpretive sign. The first time I saw the finished sign in place, it brought tears to my eyes. *"My only regret is that the last time I left Spirit Lake I didn't say good-by,"* sums up my feelings for the loss of a special friend. This is a place to reflect on the memories that we have of times spent at the Harmony Falls Lodge and the organization camps of the Columbia River Boy Scout and Girl Scout Councils, the Southwest Washington and Portland YMCA's, and the Mount St. Helens

Hiking Club. Thousands of people attended these camps each year and will treasure the friendships and new skills that were forged. These camps now lie 200 feet beneath the water of the new lake.

The background for the interpretive sign is very special as it is from a photograph of me with a Forest Service trail horse, Queen, at my favorite place on Mt. Margaret Ridge. Fortunately, this place is just as beautiful as before the eruption, and I can return often and think about the pre-eruption lake and of Queen, both of which are now gone.

Harmony Falls Trail No. 224

More difficult, 1.1 miles (one way)
Hikers only
Allow a minimum of 1.5 hours
Interpretive walks, (see Volcano Review for schedule)

This trail is the quickest access to the shoreline of the lake. It is more difficult because of the elevation change, you drop almost 1000 feet in a little more than a mile. You'll need to be careful not to slip on loose pumice on the trail on the way down, and take your time coming back up. Most people can make this hike if they use good judgment, and go at a speed that fits their physical condition. My grandson made the round trip when he was 4 years old.

You'll see interesting patterns of blown down trees and the effect that the ridge had in sheltering some trees. The wash marks left behind by the wave of water that rushed through here as a result of the landslide going into the lake are very evident. It's mind stretching to try to piece together what it must have been like.

You'll walk through patches of standing dead trees that have been stripped of all their branches and bark, and bleached white by the weather. You'll see new trees, fireweed, mountain ash, huckleberries and other plants returning to the area. If you plan wisely, you'll enjoy picking the berries as you hike back up.

Hikers follow posts that mark Harmony Falls Trail No. 224 across an area washed clean by the wave action caused when the north side of the mountain slid into Spirit Lake.

You'll be rewarded at the bottom with an excellent view of the crater and lava dome across Spirit Lake. You'll see the floating log mat, which consists of the trees that were washed into the lake by the tidal wave caused when the north side of the mountain slid into the water. Up close, you'll be surprised at the size of these tree trunks and marvel at the force it must have taken to sweep them into the lake. You'll also notice how the the wind moves them around the lake. Resist the temptation to walk on the floating logs as it would be easy to fall in the lake. How long do you think they will continue to float?

Bring along a camera with a polarizing filter and sun shade as there'll be a reflection of the sun off the water.

Look for glacial striations on the rocks at the bottom of the trail. These were exposed when the wave caused by the landslide washed this area clean. These grooves are left over from the past ice age when the Spirit Lake Basin was filled by a glacier. Rocks imbedded in the ice cut the groves as they moved along. These striations may pre-date Mount St Helens.

Independence Pass Trail No. 227 (Road 99 to Trail No. 1 at Norway Pass)

Trailhead is 4.5 miles east of Windy Ridge Viewpoint
More difficult, 3.5 miles
Hikers and mountain bikes
Elevation change from 4000 ft. to 4508 ft.

This trail begins with a steep stairway and trail for the first 1/4 mile to a good viewpoint of Mount St. Helens, the lava dome, and Spirit Lake. It continues uphill for about 3.5 miles where it junctions with Boundary Trail No.1 at Norway Pass. There are many excellent views of the mountain viewed across Spirit Lake along the route. About half way through you'll see some hummocks of mud that I believe were washed out of Spirit Lake by the wave caused by the debris avalanche and blown here by the lateral blast. A volleyball thought to be from the Portland YMCA camp was found near these hummocks.

Farther along you'll see towering rock pinnacles that were uncloaked when the lateral blast shattered and blew away the forest. Near Norway Pass you may even spot a metal boiler on the uphill side of the trail that was blown here by the blast. It appears to be a boiler that was used at the Portland YMCA Camp as a kiln for finishing pottery. Imagine the force necessary to carry this heavy metal object for several miles. There may be other artifacts from the pre-eruption Spirit Lake facilities all over this hillside. Please leave them in place and report them to the Monument Staff.

You can make this a one-way hike by parking a car at the Norway Pass Trailhead and hiking Boundary Trail No. 1 for 2.2 miles downhill to the Trailhead on Road 26, (elevation decrease of 900 feet.). There is drinking water via a hand pump at this end of the trail, and toilets.

Cascade Peaks Viewpoint

6 miles from Windy Ridge
Interpretive sign
View of three volcanoes

If you look over the hillside you can see that the area below has a young plantation of trees. This area is outside the boundary of the legislated Monument. Trees damaged by the blast were salvaged and the land reforested. It will be interesting to watch these trees grow and compare this area with adjacent areas within the Monument that are being left in order to observe natural processes.

The mountains you see in the distance are Mount Adams, Mount Hood, and Mount Rainier.

Crater House

This is a concessionaire operated food service for your convenience. They have a variety of fast foods and drinks, as well as gifts and souvenirs. There are chemical type toilets.

Meta Lake/Miners Car

Children's # 2 choice

7 miles east of Windy Ridge
Barrier-free, 1/8 mile
Hikers only
Allow 30 minutes
Drinking water via hand pump
Interpretive walks (ask for schedule)

Meta Lake Trail No. 210

The trail leaves the parking area next to the hand pump. It's an easy stroll along a paved 1/8 mile path where you can marvel at how some life survived the lateral blast by being covered by snow.

Young hiker enjoys cold well water from a hand pump at the Meta Lake Trailhead.

Notice how the beaver are damming the small stream below the trail. Watch for blue herons and ducks. At the end of the trail a viewing deck allows you to go out far enough to look into the water. Watch as thousands of tadpoles change into small frogs, as life cycles go on in this lake.

Fish were seen almost immediately after the eruption in this lake. They had large heads and small bodies indicating a lack of food. Today there is an abundance of food. The lake is open to fishing. Check with the WA Department of Wildlife for special regulations and limits.

> *The trail and viewing deck are barrier-free, but more difficult because of narrow clearing width and grades.*

Visitors at the viewing deck at Meta Lake discover why some plants and animals survived the blast.

Miner's Car

The trail continues along the road for another 1/8 mile to the miners car. This Pontiac Grand Prix was found here shortly after the eruption and is a grim reminder of the power of the lateral blast. The car was believed to have been parked on the other side of the road and was blown here, about 60 feet, by the blast. The plastic on the car seats and door trim melted but the tires survived virtually undamaged and still filled with air. In fact they looked so good that someone tried to steal them. Over the years the car has been crushed by the heavy snow pack and rusted by the weather.

Donald, Natalie, and Richard Parker, who came here in the car, were staying about one mile from here in a cabin at the Black Rock Mine on the hillside above Meta Lake. The cabin was blown away by the nearly 200 degrees F. severe winds. Only the floor remained intact, covered with over 8 inches of ash. They were found dead in their sleeping bags.

Road 99 Entrance Viewpoint

10 miles east of Windy Ridge Viewpoint
Allow 10 minutes
Interpretive signs

You're on the edge of the legislated Monument and also the edge of the 1980 lateral blast. This is a good place to visually compare the area in the Upper Clearwater Valley, that has been subjected to timber salvage and reforestation, with the area inside the Monument that has been preserved for observing the natural processes. At this point-in-time the reforested area appears much greener than the area left for nature. If you look closely at the Clearwater Valley, you can see that dead trees were left standing for wildlife habitat, and hardwood trees line the stream banks. Scientists are studying the impact of forest practices used here to learn new techniques for managing entire ecosystems across the forest.

You're also on the edge of a previous lateral blast that occurred at Mount St. Helens about 1100 years ago. The blast of May 18, 1980 was much larger and traveled three times as far. If you turn around and look directly north, you can see a fairly sharp edge to the dead trees left standing by the blast. Also, notice how the blast obeyed the stop sign.

Visitors studying interpretive signs at the edge of the dead timber from the 1980 lateral blast discover that this was also the edge of a lateral blast that occurred 1100 years ago.

Bear Meadow Viewpoint

11 miles east of Windy Ridge Viewpoint **Allow 15 minutes minimum** **Picnic tables and toilets** **Interpretive signs**

This is one viewpoint that you should visit on the way to Windy Ridge. The information about Gary Rosenquist and his famous photographs of the debris avalanche and lateral blast help set the scene for what you will see at Windy Ridge. Keith Ronnholm, a graduate student in the University of Washington Geophysics Program, was also here and took photographs. Their extraodrinary photographic documentation of the first minute of the eruption enabled scientists to reconstruct accurately what had happened.

The story related by Gary Rosenquist on the interpretive sign gives visitors an appreciation of the risk taken by those near the volcano that morning.

Boundary Trail No. 1

> **More difficult, 6 miles west to Road 26**
> **More difficult, 5 miles east to Road 25**
> **Hikers and mountain bikes west to Road 26**
> **Hikers, mountain bikes, horses and llamas west 0.25 mile to Trail No. 220 and east to Road 25**

The Bear Meadow Viewpoint and the area across the road serve as a trailhead for Boundary Trail No. 1. You can hike west on this trail as far as Coldwater Lake. There will be some restrictions in the vicinity of the construction at Johnston Ridge. Check with the Monument staff for the latest information. You can ride horses or pack llamas for about 1/4 mile west to the **Strawberry Mtn. Trail No. 220,** then ride north on Trail No. 220 for 2.5 miles to Strawberry Mtn. and some excellent views of the volcano and impacted areas. Trail No. 220 continues north for another 6.5 miles, and is described in detail later in this chapter.

You can also go east through green old-growth timber for 5 miles to Elk Pass on Road 25, or continue on for another 33 miles to Council Lake near Mount Adams. This portion of the trail is presently open to all users. The type of use permitted on portions of this trail are in the process of changing. Check with the Forest Service before taking motorized equipment.

An exciting day hike that will take a minimum of 3 hours is to go west on Trail No. 1 for 3.0 miles to **Ghost Lake Trail No. 1H,** and then north on Trail No. 1H for 0.4 mile to the lake. This is a good example of the impact that the blast and ashfall had on the backcountry lakes. This is also an excellent hike for picking huckleberries.

Wakapish Sno-Park

> **17 miles to Windy Ridge**
> **20 miles to Randle**
> **Toilets and warming shelter**

This Sno-Park is a good place to drop off your trailer or recreation vehicle so you don't need to take it all the way to Windy Ridge. The winter use of this Sno-Park will be discussed in Chapter 8.

Iron Creek Falls Trail No. 91

More difficult, 0.5 mile
Hikers only

About halfway between Road 2516 and Road 99 (a distance of one mile) on Road 25, you'll find a small parking area for the Iron Creek Falls Trail No. 91. You can park here and walk down the trail for only 0.5 mile to a good viewpoint of this 60 foot waterfall. The Forest Service should have a sign along the road by the time you read this book. It's a nice stop if you can plan an extra 15 minutes into your visit to the mountain.

Strawberry Mtn. Viewpoint

Eighteen miles south of Randle take Road 2516, drive 10 miles to the end of the gravel surfaced road to the edge of the blast area. The Forest Service has provided interpretive signs that tell about the fire lookout that once stood on top of Strawberry Peak. Today most of the lookout towers are gone with most fire detection being done from aircraft and satellites.

A fire lookout guard had an interesting summer of solitude, often having to hike many miles to the nearest road, and being out of contact with others for weeks. Many of us think we would gladly swap our busy lifestyle of today for the peace and quiet of the fire lookout. It's possible to experience the life of the lookout as a volunteer. Check with a Forest Service office near you for more information.

Strawberry Mtn. Trail No. 220

> **More difficult, 2.5 miles south from Road 2516 to Trail No. 1 and 6.5 miles north to Road 2600045**
> **Hikers, mountain bikes, horses and llamas**

One mile prior to the viewpoint at the end of Road 2516, Trail No. 220 crosses the road.

If you take the trail to the south, you'll climb for one mile to the top of Strawberry Peak, elevation 5464 feet. This is where the lookout building was located. The views of Mount St. Helens, the crater, and blast area are exceptional. Mount Adams, Mount Rainier, and Mount Hood are also visible.

If you continue south for 1.5 miles more you'll join the Boundary Trail No. 1 about 1/4 mile from Bear Meadow Viewpoint at an elevation of 4000 feet. Most of the trip from the peak is in green timber. If you can work it out to leave a vehicle at Bear Meadow and get a ride to the end of Road 2516, your life will be more enjoyable. The 1500 foot elevation change makes this a more difficult trail.

If you go north on the trail you'll follow the ridge top that is the border between the blast killed forest and live forest. At places along the trail the standing dead trees bleached white by the sun make interesting frames for your photographs. The trail continues north through sub-alpine meadows filled with Indian Paint Brush and Harebells. The trail enters green forest and passes above two picturesque small lakes. It drops down through the forest and ends in some recently logged areas. I recommend that you turn around at the area above the lakes as you've seen the best scenery and the trail descends very steeply.

This area is outside the Monument. Mountain bikers have commented that the trail is extremely difficult and that the ash creates a problem with the gears.

Iron Creek Campground & Picnic Area

> **27 miles to Windy Ridge**
> **10 miles to Randle**
> **98 camping units, group picnicking**
> **Barrier-free trails**

This is a handy place to camp when visiting this part of the Monument. The coolness of the old-growth will feel good after spending all day in the treeless blast impacted area. On the weekend you'll enjoy campfire programs.

The camping will cost $9.00 a night for a single unit and $14.00 a night for a double unit. Reservations are available through MISTIX by calling 1-800-283-CAMP. There are usually presentations in the amphitheater on weekend evenings during the summer. There is more information presented about this campground in Chapter 10.

Iron Creek Campground Loop Trail No. 187

> **Barrier-free, 1.5 miles**
> **Hikers only**

This recently restored trail provides barrier-free access around the campground and ties into a new interpretive trail in the Iron Creek Picnic Area. It's a wonderful place to view old-growth Douglas-fir. The ages of some trees were signed by the Civilian Conservation Corps.

Iron Creek Picnic Area Trail No. 89

> **Barrier-free, 0.2 mile**
> **Hikers only**
> **Giant old-growth trees**

If you're interested in old-growth timber, take the 0.2 mile barrier-free interpretive trail in the picnic area and learn about 600 year old trees. This trail is at the 1200 foot elevation and available for most of the year. The hardwood trees mixed into the understory make it a beautiful place to visit in the fall. Several interpretive signs explain the ecology of old-growth timber. This trail ties into the Campground Loop Trail No. 187 that allows an additional 1.5 miles of barrier-free experience.

> *This interpretive trail is a more difficult barrier-free because of the gravel surface and clearing width, but it is suitable for wheelchairs. It may be combined with the Campground Loop Trail or a trip to Quartz Creek Big Trees Interpretive Trail to make a day of barrier-free old-growth experiences.*

Visitors discover that hugging a 600 year old tree is not easy.

Woods Creek Information Station

31 miles east of Windy Ridge
6 miles south of Randle on Road 25
Open daily May 18 to Sept. 30, 9 a.m. to 5 p.m.

You can either have your questions answered at a drive-up window without leaving your car or go inside and visit with an interpreter and look at displays. Maps, books, brochures, video tapes and slides are for sale. There is a picnic area with additional restrooms and drinking water across Road 25 from the information station. This area was developed for watching for signs of wildlife. There is a barrier-free trail around a beaver pond and interpretive signs to help you identify what you see.

Boundary Trail No. 1 Trailhead at Elk Pass

> **More difficult, 33 miles east to Council Lake**
> **More difficult, 5 miles west to Bear Meadow**
> **Hikers, mountain bikes, horses, llamas and motor bikes**

This is a National Recreation Trail that is also the major east/west trail on the Gifford Pinchot National Forest. If you go east from here for about 33 miles you'll arrive at Council Lake near Mount Adams. This portion of the trail is open to all types of use today, but, check with the Forest Service before taking motorized equipment as the situation is going to change in the near future. If you go west, you'll find Bear Meadow Viewpoint on Road 99 at about 5 miles, Norway Pass Trailhead on Road 26 at 9.5 miles, Truman Trail No. 207 at 17 miles, and Coldwater Lake at 24 miles.

This trail follows the ridge that divides the Cowlitz River Watershed from the Lewis River Watershed. A few miles to the east the trail enters the Dark Divide Roadless Area, one of the largest remaining roadless areas on the west side of the Cascade Mountains that has not been classified as Wilderness. This trail, which had to be restored from the 8 to 10 inches of new ash after the eruption, provides wonderful vistas of the Gifford Pinchot National Forest.

It's name came from the fact that this ridge was the southern boundary of the Mount Rainier National Forest Reserve before the area was divided into the National Park and the National Forest. It follows one of the major Native American travel routes.

Clearwater Viewpoint

> **26 miles to Windy Ridge Viewpoint**
> **36 miles to Cougar**
> **Allow 5 minutes**

You'll have an opportunity for a closer look at the Upper Clearwater Valley where the Forest Service has salvaged the trees killed by the volcano and replanted the area. Notice how some of the trees have been left to provide habitat for wildlife, and how hardwoods were planted along the stream to provide shade and a food source. It's estimated that the trees salvaged here have built 50,000 houses. The more severely shattered trees were run through large chippers, brought here to the valley, and hauled to the mills for processing into paper and fiberboard.

Muddy River Viewpoint

37 miles to Windy Ridge
25 miles to Cougar
Allow 5 minutes

Although this area looks like a young alder forest, it is worth the few minutes it takes to read the interpretive signs and realize the depth and volume of mud that roared past here on May 18, 1980. The depth of the mud is documented by a white stripe at the top of a pole near the sign. The 1980 mudflows are very small when compared to others that have shaped the landscape in this area. Most of the forest that you drive through between here and Cougar is growing on old mudfows.

Cedar Flats Nature Trail No. 32

38 miles to Windy Ridge
24 miles to Cougar
More difficult barrier-free, 1 mile loop trail
Hikers only, good for children
Allow 1 hour minimum

Early day foresters recognized the value of this outstanding area of old-growth western red cedar and Douglas-fir, and set it aside for research in the 1930's. In 1946, 680 acres were designated as a Research Natural Area to study the natural processes. Many of these Douglas-fir and cedar trees tower over 200 feet tall and are over 30 feet in circumference. They serve as an excellent example of the productivity of mudflow material from Mount St.

Helens. It's extremely important that you stay on the trail to protect the research potential. About half way through the loop portion of the trail there is a good view of the Muddy River.

This natural surface trail is level and has wide clearing. It is accessible to wheelchairs but is a challenge. The first 100 feet are the steepest. Parking and unloading may be a problem. It's a great trail for small children.

Pine Creek Viewpoint

21 miles to Cougar
41 miles to Windy Ridge
Interpretive sign gives the ingredients for a mudflow

On May 18, 1980 a 30 foot wall of mud about the consistency of wet cement roared through this stream channel at about 40 mph. It stripped all the vegetation from along the stream bank and ripped a concrete bridge from its foundation. This mudflow and accumulation of debris joined with the mudflow from the Muddy River just below here in the Lewis River. It then flowed into Swift Reservoir destroying the major concrete bridge on Road 90 enroute. The mud turned the water of the reservoir into a dark brown brew which blocked-out light and suffocated all fish life. When corralled by the Pacific Power and Light Company, the floating woody debris covered about 18 acres of the surface. The debris was sold by the Forest Service for timber salvage and removed from the reservoir at the boat launch at Swift Forest Camp.

On May 19, when Forest Service employees returned to this site, they found a 40 ton boulder deposited by the mudflow in the middle of the road. This huge rock was moved to the downhill side of the road and is a testimony to the power of a mudflow. Upstream, mud lines on some of the surviving trees document the height of this mudflow. There's a short trail that provides foot access to the Lewis River.

Pine Creek Information Station

42 miles to Windy Ridge
20 miles to Cougar
Barrier-free toilets and displays

This information station is described in Chapter 1. In addition to the information station the Forest Service has a work center operating here for about 10 months out of the year. This is an old mudflow that is much larger than the 1980 mudlow. The Geological Survey scientists were concerned before 1980 that a large mudflow could reoccur sweeping the former ranger station and surrounding forest into the reservoir, a nerve-wrecking thought for those working there. This could cause a massive displacement of water, overtopping the Swift Dam, causing a major flooding disaster in the Lewis River. Fortunately, this didn't happen in 1980. The glaciers have melted and the possibility is diminished for the present.

Mount St. Helens Trivia

It's evident that Native Americans recognized the eruptive nature of the mountain by the names that they gave to it such as:

Loowit, "Keeper of the Fire"

Lawelatha, "One from Who Smoke Comes"

Tah-One-Lat-Clah, "Fire Mountain"

Captain George Vancouver of the British Royal Navy named Mount St. Helens in 1792 in honor of Alleyne Fitzherbert, who held the title Baron St. Helens and who was at that time the British Ambassador to Spain. Fitzherbert was the key negotiator on a treaty with Spain that had opened the Pacific Coast to British exploration.

Chapter 4 Lava and Mudflows, South & West Sides of Mount St. Helens

For more detailed maps for trails use USGS Quads E16.2, E17.1 and E17.2

The best access to the mudflows and lava flows on the south and west sides of Mount St. Helens is to take Exit 21 on Interstate 5 at Woodland and drive east on SR 503 to Jack's Restaurant, about 23 miles. The main SR 503 turns south to Amboy, and a spur of SR 503 continues east through the town of Cougar, which is about 5 more miles. Jack's is an important landmark in the area, and is especially important if you plan to climb the mountain as it's where you register for your climb.

About 2 miles east you'll see a road sign that reads to tune to 530 on your car AM radio for volcano information. This short range radio station repeats information on the road conditions and is particularly useful in the winter for getting updated on snow conditions and avalanche hazards.

In Cougar you'll find Bluebird Helicopter Service. For about $65.00 per person they'll give you a 30 minute helicopter tour to the north side of the mountain where you can look right into the crater and get an overview of the vast area impacted by the blast. You'll need to make reservations ahead as they require a minimum of three people per flight and need to have it scheduled.

This is the last chance for gas and food. The people working in the stores are usually well informed about the south side volcanic attractions and enjoy sharing this information with visitors. Stop and top off your gas tank and pick up a few snacks for replacing some of the energy you'll be burning off.

Continue east on Spur SR 503 for about one mile where Cougar Creek flows under the road. If it's September or early October, stop and look into the stream for spawning Kokanee Salmon. You'll know immediately if the fish are there because of the bright red color of their bodies. The Pacific Power and Light Company's Cougar and Beaver Bay Campgrounds along here are perfect for supporting overnight trips to this part of the Monument. There is more information on these camps in Chapter 10.

About 3.5 miles from Cougar, Spur SR 503 will turn into Forest Service Road 90. Although this is an asphalt paved road that looks almost identical to the state highway, it is not designed for the same 55 miles per hour speed. Watch closely for speed limit and approaching curve signs. If you're pulling a trailer or are traveling slower than the other traffic, use the slow vehicle turnouts to allow traffic to pass you. Watch for logging trucks and heavy equipment. If you have a CB radio, tune to the channel recommended for this route.

Road 83 Access

About 8 miles east of Cougar you'll find Road 83 taking off to the left. Drive north on it for about 2 miles to the Junction of Road 8303. Turn left and proceed about one mile to Ape Cave Interpretive Site.

Ape Cave Interpretive Site

Children and/or groups # 1 Choice

11 miles to Cougar
2 miles long cave
Lamps available on site for $3.00
Wear warm clothing
Allow 2 hours minimum
Elevation 2200 ft.
Guided lantern tours available

At 12,810 feet long, Ape Cave is the longest known intact unitary lava tube in the continental United States. If you haven't hiked at least the lower portion of this cave, you're missing one of the best experiences available anywhere in the northwest. The lower end is suitable for children, and it's a great opportunity to introduce them to caves.

A group of cave explorers use team work to overcome the nine foot high lava fall in the upper portion of Ape Cave.

At the parking area is the Ape's Headquarters where you can rent a propane or battery operated lamp. You'll need to leave a driver's license and pay $3.00 for each lamp. You can also buy an assortment of books, slides, and other information appropriate to the lava flow and caves. This information building is open from about May 1 to Sept. 30. It's hours are 10 am to 6 pm daily.

A 300 foot barrier-free trail leads to the lower entrance of the cave. An information kiosk explains the lava flow that formed the cave approximately 1900 years ago, the discovery and exploration, and the fragile life that struggles for survival in the cave. It also points out the equipment and clothing needed for enjoying a safe visit. It suggests that you bring at least two sources of light:

- A propane or gas lantern to provide light to view cave features and to light your footing.
- A flashlight with strong batteries can be used to spotlight specific features and be available as a backup light in case the lantern fails.

The temperature in the cave stays near 42 degrees F all year. Wear long pants, a sweater or jacket, and sturdy shoes.

Lower Cave

Ape cave is divided into two sections, upslope and downslope, from this entrance. The downslope portion extends about 4000 feet and ends in a sand fill. It's fairly easy hiking and suitable for small children. As you descend the stairway into the cave, continue straight ahead when you reach the bottom and you'll be headed into the downslope portion.

In this portion of the cave there is a Lava Ball, a block of solidified lava which was carried along in the lava stream and became wedged in a narrow portion of the passage. You will also see lateral lava flow marks along the walls. When the lava level dropped and stabilized for a period of time, a flow mark was produced along the wall.

Upper Cave

When you reach the bottom of the stairway, if you turn to your left and go back under the stairs, you'll be headed into the upslope portion of the cave. This passage extends about 8000 feet and is very difficult to travel.

Fortunately, it's possible to exit the cave near the upper end and return to the parking area on a 1.25 miles trail on the surface. The **Ape Cave Trail No. 239** follows along the surface of the lava flow back to the lower entrance.

There's a lot of breakdown in this section of the cave. Breakdown is the rock rubble caused by the collapse of the passage walls and ceiling. At two places in the upper cave this breakdown extends to the surface forming entrances. The Forest Service has provided a steel ladder at the uppermost entrance so visitors can return above ground.

The breakdown provides narrow passages and a lot of climbing. At one point there is a Lava Falls that is about 9 feet high. These natural barriers will provide you with plenty of challenge. Allow 3 to 4 hours for a round trip of this end of the cave.

Impact of the 1980 Eruptions

There were no lava flows during the most recent series of eruptions, and no breakdown caused by the earthquakes. However, Ape Cave was threatened by ash, pumice and sand that was transported in surface water run-off during heavy rain storms in November and December of 1980. After one small lava tube was observed by scientists to rapidly fill, the Forest Service decided to protect Ape Cave and another cave from these alluvial flows. This was done by filling sand bags with the material and diverting the flow away from the cave entrances. You can still see evidence of these alluvial flows along Road 8303, especially in the area around the Trail of Two Forests, and along Road 81.

The Oregon Grotto of the National Speleological Society has been a longtime partner with the Gifford Pinchot National Forest and they maintain the trail and print an Ape Cave brochure. Anyone interested in learning more about these lava tubes should write to: Oregon Grotto of the National Speleological Society, 912 N.W. 50th Street, Vancouver, WA 98663.

Ape Cave is designated as a National Recreation Trail because of the unusual recreation experience it offers.

Trail of Two Forests Interpretive Trail No. 233

Children & Barrier-free #1 Choice

1 mile from Ape Cave on Road 8303
Barrier-free, easiest, 0.25 mile
Hikers only
Allow one hour
Elevation 1810 ft.

This is an excellent hiking interpretive opportunity, especially when linked with a trip to Ape Cave.

It is an easy, barrier-free trail that is built as a boardwalk and is accessible to everyone. It is the easiest wheelchair access on the Gifford Pinchot National Forest. The toilets and picnic area are also barrier-free.

It is the best children's trail in the Monument. Your child will love crawling through the cool dark interior of a horizontal tree mold. A flashlight will help with the first crawl through. Then, you may have a problem getting the kids to stop after ten or more trips through the mold.

This interesting geologic area was formerly know as the Lava Cast Picnic Area. As the interpretive signs were being written, it became clear that the interesting forms left after the lava flowed around the former forest were really molds. These signs will help you understand the 1900 year-old lava flow that created these tree molds and the adjacent lava tubes. Life is a struggle for new plants attempting to live here, so stay on the trail and give these plants the best chance possible. There is a small picnic area. Bring along a picnic lunch and enjoy the coolness of the new forest.

The combination of Ape Cave and the Trail of Two Forests present an excellent opportunity for a field trip for students in the Portland/Vancouver area. Contact the Gifford Pinchot National Forest for sources of environmental learning packets in advance of your trip.

Marble Mountain Sno-Park

About 4.5 miles east of Road 8303 Jct.
Group picnicking facility by reservation
Emergency telephone, toilets
Elevation 2700 ft.

Continue on the newly paved double-lane Road 83 for another 4.5 miles to the Marble Mountain Sno-Park. You are now 13 miles northeast of Cougar. The area you have just driven through is an extensive old mudflow that extends all the way to the new mudflow at the end of this road.

The primary function of this facility is a warming hut and trailhead for winter trail use. The winter use will be discussed in Chapter 8.

During the summer months the gate is kept locked but the shelter can be rented by groups for special events. The warming hut has tables to accommodate approximately 50 people. It could provide a good sheltered eating experience on a rainy day for school or other group tours. There is no overnight camping. Call or write the Monument Headquarters in Amboy, (206) 247-5473, to reserve the shelter.

Most early-season mountain climbing originates here because road access to the best climbing route is blocked by snow until about June. There is a solar operated emergency telephone. This is discussed in more detail in the next chapter.

June Lake Trail No. 216B

More difficult, 1.4 miles to Trail No. 216
Hikers, mountain bikes and cross-country skiers
Elevation change from 3160 ft. to 3400 ft.

Turn left about 14 miles northeast of Cougar and drive about 250 feet to a small trailhead parking area. The first 0.5 mile of the trail is through a young timber stand plantation that was established after the timber was harvested. The trail follows along June Lake Creek and has some good photo opportunities of the mountain with the stream in the foreground.

Continue on for about one mile to June Lake. The sandy beach and dead trees on the open west side of the lake are the result of ash being washed down the mountain slopes in the fall of 1980. A good portion of the lake silted in but has recovered. The waterfalls flowing over the cliffs that surround the lake provide excellent photo opportunities if you wait for a mirror surface on the water. This is an excellent family hike.

Above June Lake the trail gets steep and most difficult until it joins the Loowit Trail No. 216. The only potential potable water is located in Short Creek near Trail No. 216. This stream flows out of an old lava flow, runs on the surface for about 200 feet, and disappears into the lava. It is not being tested, but sure tasted good to thirsty travelers on a long journey around the mountain. Use at your own risk.

Experienced hikers can make extended trips either east or west on the **Loowit Trail No. 216.** Although the Loowit Trail No. 216 is open to mountain bikes it is only recommended to those bikers willing to carry their bikes for long distances over rock terrain.

Pine Creek Shelter Trail No. 216C

17 miles NE of Cougar on Road 83 **Easiest, 0.4 miles** **Hikers, mountain bikes and cross-country skiers** **Elevation change from 2980 ft. to 3100 ft.**

This trail provided a link to Spirit Lake prior to being wiped off the landscape by a mudflow in 1980. Today it provides access to the Jackpine Shelter. This rustic structure, constructed in 1932, was recently restored by the Quintin Robbin's family, Roy Campbell, Jim McDonald and Ralph Bozarth. You also can be a partner with the Forest Service on similar type projects. Contact the Monument Headquarters for information.

The shelter is open to anyone. It's very popular in the winter with skiers, but also provides protection for summertime backpackers. You'll walk through an old-growth noble fir forest, and have some outstanding views of Mount St. Helens. It's a nice hike for children.

Lahar Recreation Area

17.5 miles NE of Cougar on Road 83
Open June through October

You're about to enter onto the mudflow that occurred in 1980 on the Muddy River and Pine Creek. There are several developed trails and viewpoints to help you see and understand this area. These are as follows:

Lahar Trail No. 241

Easiest, barrier-free, 0.1 mile
Interpretive sign

Turn right into a small paved parking area and take a short trail to a viewpoint and sign. Notice how the mudflow has stripped the bark from the large trees nearby. Imagine what it was like with mud flowing through here to a depth of 30 feet. Toward the mountain you'll see a bare ridge where the mud scraped off all vegetation as it slammed into and ran over the ridge. You can see Mount Hood, Mount Rainier, Mount Adams and Mount St. Helens.

The trail is barrier-free and winds along the mudflow allowing you to see small plants recolonizing the area.

Barrier-free trails allow visitors to explore the Muddy River Mudflow.

Moss Springs Viewpoint

17.6 miles from Cougar on Road 83
Interpretive sign

A short distance beyond the Lahar Viewpoint turn right into a small parking area. Prior to the 1980 mudflow this area was covered with old growth noble fir. Moss Springs was a popular place to stop for a cold drink of water and to refill your water jugs. It was a welcome sight to find the spring bubbling out of the earth after the mudfow in 1980. A poem reflects on the value of spring water to our lives.

Do not bring your trailer or RV into this short narrow road as you may not be able to turn around.

Stratigraphy Viewpoint

17.7 miles from Cougar on Road 83
Interpretive sign

On the left side of the road just a short distance from the Lahar Viewpoint is an interesting sight. The recent mudflow removed vegetation and cut into the hillside exposing different colored and textured layers of volcanic deposits that occurred here over the past 13,000 years. You can easily see how active Mount St. Helens has been in building this portion of the mountain. The sign compares these layers to pages in a diary.

Lava Canyon Trail No. 184

Authors Hiking # 1 choice

18 miles from Cougar on Road 83
Barrier-free, 0.5 mile
More difficult, 0.2 mile
Most difficult, (treacherous) 1.7 miles
Hikers only
Elevation change from 2900 ft. to 1580 ft.
Allow 2 hours minimum

This is one of the most interesting trails in the Monument. The 1980 mudflows scoured all the vegetation and soil from this canyon revealing a 1900 year old lava flow. The Muddy River flows through interesting lava formations making for interesting photo opportunities.

The trailhead and picnic area are at the end of Road 83. Barrier-free composting toilets provide sanitation and interest.

The first 0.5 mile of the trail are barrier-free with a paved asphalt surface. The grade is near 7% for almost all of the 0.5 mile, and it is a more difficult trail for wheelchair use. The trail is about 4 feet wide with occasional wider areas for wheelchairs to pass. There are short breaks in the grade for rest stops on the climb out.

The view of several waterfalls in the rocky canyon make the experience worth the challenge of the climb on the return trip. There are interpretive signs and viewing decks on this portion of the trail and rustic benches for resting during your ascent. This portion of the trail is great for children but don't let them get ahead of you as the trail runs along the edge of a cliff just beyond the viewing area at the end of the paved trail.

Lava Canyon Trail allows visitors to come close to the river and feel the spray and hear the roar of the water.

Near this viewing area, **Trail No. 184A** takes off to the right and follows an interesting lava trough before crossing the Muddy River. Children need to be well supervised as there is the danger of falling into the river and being swept over a waterfall. The bridge is located directly below a waterfall and the roar of the rushing water gives you a special feeling. A few hundred feet farther and the trail descends a cliff via a metal stairway, it then takes you along basalt cliffs to the location of a proposed suspension bridge to be constructed in 1993. When completed, this bridge will allow you to make a loop trip of about 0.5 mile, and view the canyon from both sides. The 110 foot long bridge will provide Indiana Jones type excitement as you look down 100 feet to the top of a waterfall.

If you continue on past the viewpoint at the end of the barrier-free trail, you'll see signs warning you that the trail becomes more difficult and that there are cliffs. After about 0.1 mile you'll pass the east end of the proposed suspension bridge. Only experienced hikers should go below this point. A sign warns that the trail is dangerous. If you have a fear of heights you will have trouble the first time through the next 0.5 mile of trail.

The trail drops about 1200 feet in elevation in the next mile, and I recommend that you park a car at the lower trailhead so you won't have to climb out of this hole. Take gravel surfaced Road 8322 at the road junction about 200 feet west of the Lahar Viewpoint. Proceed downhill to the east for about 6 miles to a parking area near the confluence of Smith Creek and the Muddy River. Smith Creek Trail No. 225 takes off from here, crossing the Muddy River on a long steel bridge. About 200 feet north of the bridge, the Lava Canyon Trail No. 184 joins this trail on the left.

As you hike down the trail be careful of your footing as the trail surface is steep. If you fall off the trail you could be seriously injured. You pass a wet area that has a cable installed on the uphill side. The wet trail surface is slippery. This is the only safety cable on the trail. You'll see several other small streams along the trail. All surface water is unsafe to drink. Carry lots of drinking water, you'll be working hard and will need it.

If you look across the canyon you'll see some dead trees with the bark scraped off. This provides evidence of the level of the mudflow as it passed through this canyon. The alder trees growing along the stream have all started growing there since 1980.

The trail takes you close to the stream where you can hear the sound and feel the spray. At one point you pass water running through a lava trough. A dead tree trapped vertically in the waterfall at the bottom end of the trough wiggles to the rhythm of the water. A 50 foot spur trail takes you to a viewpoint of several waterfalls that you have hiked past.

A little farther on you pass beneath the lava cliffs which are giants columns of basalt. Some of the rock has been falling apart and makes a hard surface for the trail. About 0.75 mile below the start of the most difficult trail you'll come to the top of a cliff. A steel, 30 foot, ladder allows you to continue.

The heavy shadows in the canyon make it necessary to use a good flash for photos of the ladder. The morning lighting is best for photographing the waterfalls.

Continue on for another 0.25 mile where you'll come upon an intersection. Turn right on Ship Trail No. 184B and climb the ladder and steep trail onto the lava formation called The Ship. It's about 0.25 mile to an excellent viewpoint at the upper end of the rock.

If you parked a vehicle at the lower trailhead, continue on down the main trail along the Muddy River for about another full mile. If you return up the trail you'll agree with some of the descriptions used by my grandchildren when we did the return trip: heart pounding, grueling, cruelly steep, punishing, exciting, torturing and scary.

Ape Canyon Trail No. 234

Mountain bikers # 1 choice

More difficult, 5.5 miles
Hikers and mountain bikes
Elevation change from 2930 ft. to 4140 ft.

As you leave the Lava Canyon Trailhead, you'll notice a small parking area on the north side of Road 83. This is the trailhead for Ape Canyon Trail No. 234. This trail follows along the edge of the mudflow, mostly in the timber, and provides some excellent views of the mountain. At about 5.5 miles it joins the Loowit Trail No. 216 at Ape Canyon.

This is a particularly interesting location with a view between the cliffs that form Ape Canyon down into the valley. You can almost relive the mud flow pouring through this narrow canyon.

The canyon gets its name from a story, from the 1930's, about several miners staying in a cabin near here. During the night, ape-like creatures hurled boulders onto the cabin from above. There have been several other stories of ape-man type sightings in the Spirit Lake area over the years, and numerous hunting expeditions in search of them. These stories, coincidentally, started about the same time youth camps and Civilian Conservation Corps camps were first developing at Spirit Lake.

This trail when combined with Loowit Trail Segment No. 216.6, (1.8 miles), Abraham Trail No. 216D, (1.75 miles), and a portion of Truman Trail No. 207, (1.75 miles), makes an excellent 10.8 mile hike or mountain bike trip between Windy Ridge and Road 83.

Merrill Lake Road No. 81

The other principle road into the south and west sides of the mountain is Road 81. It takes off of Spur SR 503 about one mile west of Cougar and goes north through private timberlands. Near the road junction on SR 503 you'll see a Forest Service log scaling station. All timber that is harvested on the National Forest is measured to determine payment. At this location the logs are measured while on the trucks. As you drive this road watch out for logging trucks coming downhill. Give them the right-of-way as a loaded truck is very difficult to stop.

This road connects with Road 83 after 16 miles. By returning on Road 83 via Road 90 to Cougar you can have an enjoyable 27 mile drive through this part of the Monument. Some of the points of interest along this route are described below.

Merrill Lake Campground

4.7 miles from Cougar
11 campsites for tents or small trailers
Boat launch and fly fishing

This campground, operated by the Washington State Dept. of Natural Resources, has no fee and no reservations. The lake was formed about 2000 years ago by a lava flow from the mountain. There is more information on this campground in Chapter 10.

Gifford Pinchot National Forest Entrance

At about 7.4 miles from SR 503 you'll see the National Forest entrance sign. Notice the lodgepole pine timber growing in this area. Where you see this, it indicates an old pyroclastic flow occurred about 500 years ago.

Kalama Horse Camp

8.7 miles from SR 503
Major trailhead for Trail No. 238
10 campsites, no fee
Open May through Oct.

This campground was constructed by volunteers from the Backcountry Horsemen of WA, the WA Trail Riders Assoc., and the Clark County Executive Horse Council, and assisted with funding from WA State Interagency Committee for Outdoor Recreation. If you use the facilities please give a thank you to the folks you see here with horses as they probably were involved with the work.

The facilities are barrier-free and include a ramp for mounting onto horses.

Mosquitoes and flies are numerous before late June. You should avoid camping here until mid-summer or later. The water here is for the livestock only.

There is parking for 20 vehicles and trailers at the trailhead for the Toutle River Trail No. 238.

Toutle Trail No. 238.1, (Kalama Horse Camp to Road 600)

Easy, 3.8 miles
Hikers, mountain bikes, horses, llamas and cross-country skiers
Elevation change from 2068 ft. to 2600 ft.

This trail follows along the steep bank of the north side of the Toutle River for 3.8 miles to Road 600. It provides good access for fishing and hunting, and provides a trail tie to approximately 20 miles of horse trails to the north.

Blue Lake Horse Trail No. 237.1, (Trail No. 238 to Trail No. 238)

> **Easy, 2.8 miles**
> **Hikers, mountain bikes, horses, llamas and cross-country skiers**
> **Elevation change from 2600 ft. to 3280 ft.**

If you want to travel north, take Blue Lake Horse Trail No. 237.1, which is on Road 600, for the first 0.3 mile to Road 81. Thereafter it goes north through a lodgepole pine forest to provide loop trail opportunities. It intersects Segment 4 of the Toutle River Trail No. 238 after 2.8 miles.

Toutle Trail No. 238.2, (Road 600 to Red Rock Pass)

> **More difficult, 1.8 miles**
> **Hikers, mountain bikers, horses, llamas, cross-country skiers**
> **Elevation change from 2600 ft. to 3116 ft.**

You can continue east on the Toutle Trail No. 238.2 from Road 600 to Road 81 at Red Rock Pass. You'll pass on the south shore of McBride Lake, a five acre pond that provides a good trout fishing opportunity.

Toutle Trail No. 238.3, (Red Rock Pass to Trail No. 238A)

> **More difficult, 1.2 miles**
> **Hikers, mountain bikes, horses, llamas and cross-country skiers**
> **Elevation change from 3116 ft. to 3520 ft.**

This trail begins at Red Rock Pass Trailhead on Road 81 about 13.5 miles from SR 503. There are some very interesting views of the mountain across the lava flow in the first 0.2 mile. This part of the trail is gravel surfaced on top of the lava and is a good place to take children. The upper part of this trail is most difficult for cross-country skiing.

Trails across lava flows provide unsual experiences for visitors.

The Toutle Trail No. 238.4 turns west and Butte Camp Trail No. 238A goes north to the Loowit Trail No. 216 at timberline. Trails No. 238A and Trail No. 216 are discussed in Chapter 5.

Toutle Trail No. 238.4, (Trail No. 238A to Blue Lake Trailhead)

More difficult, 2.2 miles
Hikers, mountain bikes, horses, llamas and cross-country skiers
Elevation change from 3520 ft. to 3225 ft.

The trail goes east through a noble fir forest on the slope below Butte Camp and crosses a mudflow from 1980. There are excellent views of the mountain while in the openings created by the mudflow. In a stand of young lodgepole pine the trail intersects with the Blue Lake Horse Trail No. 237 at 1.9 miles. This allows you to make a short loop trip of about 15 miles back to Trail No. 238 and the Horse Camp.

(Merrill Lake Road 81 discussion continued)-
As you exit the Kalama Horse Camp and turn east, the paved road narrows to single lane. The pavement ends after another 2.2 miles and the road is single-lane with gravel surface.

Road 8123 Blue Lake Trailhead

| 13 miles from Cougar |

At 11.4 miles from SR 503 you'll arrive at the junction of Road 81 and Road 8123. If you want to go to the west side of the mountain take Road 8123. This trailhead which puts you in the middle of the Toutle River Trail No. 238 and Blue Lake Horse Trail No. 237 is only 1.7 miles from the junction of Road 81 and Road 8123.

Toutle River Trail No. 238.5 and 238.6, (Road 8123 to Trail No. 240)

> **Easy, 0.2 mile to Blue Lake**
> **More difficult, 3.0 miles to Sheep Canyon**
> **Hikers, mountain bikes, horses and llamas**
> **Elevation change from 3225 ft. to 3950 ft.**

Trail No. 238.5 goes north past Blue Lake after 0.2 mile and passes through some outstanding old-growth noble fir. If you're quiet, alert and lucky, you may see deer, elk or black bear along this section of the trail. If you continue on for 3 miles you'll intersect Sheep Canyon Trail No. 240 and can follow it for 0.7 mile to the Sheep Canyon Trailhead. You could also take off on Trail No. 237 at 2.3 miles and make a round trip of about 5 miles.

Blue Lake Horse Trail No. 237.2 (Trail No. 238 to Trail No. 238)

> **More Difficult, 2.5 miles**
> **Hikers, mountain bikes, horses and llamas**
> **Elevation change from 3280 ft. to 3900 ft.**

Starting from the Sheep Canyon end on Trail No. 238.5 this trail goes through a young plantation of noble fir, crosses the headwaters of Coldsprings Creek, and eventually into a unique stand of large old-growth noble fir. You'll climb to a viewpoint on a 1980 mudflow and have an outstanding view of Mount St. Helens.

(Road 8123 discussion continued)-

From the Blue Lake Trailhead continue northwest on Road 8123. If you look to the southwest you'll see Goat Mountain with Goat Marsh in the foreground. Continue for 4.8 miles to where the road ends at Sheep Canyon Viewpoint.

Sheep Canyon Viewpoint & Trailhead

17.9 miles from SR 503
More difficult, 0.3 mile trail to a good viewpoint

You're at the southern edge of the 1980 lateral blast. Take the short trail through a noble fir forest to a good viewpoint of the South Fork of the Toutle River and try to imagine the blast and mudflow that occurred a short distance away. The hillside across the river has been salvaged by private land owners and the state. This parking area also serves trail users to the slopes of the mountain and Castle Lake via the following trails.

Trail-riders on the Blue Lake Horse Trail No. 237 enjoy beautiful scenery and tall noble fir trees while learning about the eruptions that changed this area in 1980 . (Photo by Lorri Bisconer)

Sheep Canyon Trail No. 240

> **More difficult 2.3 miles to Loowit Trail No. 216**
> **Hikers and mountain bikes, 2.3 miles**
> **Horses and llamas, 0.7 mile**
> **Elevation change from 3420 ft. to 4600 ft.**

This trail provides a variety of views within a short distance of road access. The first segment of 0.7 mile to the Toutle Trail No. 238 crossing is open to horses, llamas, mountain bikes, and hikers. This allows this trailhead to serve the extensive system of horse trails on the west side of the mountain. The trail begins in a young noble fir plantation and soon climbs through an old growth stand of noble firs. Just before it crosses Trail No. 238 you get a good view of Sheep Canyon and a 75 foot waterfall. To the west you'll see the gray colored blast area.

The trail continues along Sheep Canyon Creek for another 1.6 miles to the Loowit Trail No. 216. This portion of the trail is open only for hikers and mouintain bikers. You can go north or south on Trail No. 216 and make loops. These are discussed in Chapter 5.

Sheep Canyon is a steep white-gray colored drainage that was deepened by major run-off from melting glaciers in 1980. The higher the trail climbs the shorter the trees become. It joins Trail No. 216 near timberline. Normally timberline is at about 6000 feet in this part of the region, but because of Mount St. Helens continuous volcanic activity it is around 4500 feet here.

Toutle Trail No. 238.7, (Trail No. 240 to Trail No. 216)

> **More difficult, 1.5 miles**
> **Hikers and mountain bikes**
> **Elevation change from 3540 ft. to 3250 ft.**

Turn left off Trail No. 240 at Sheep Canyon Creek and cross the canyon on a bridge upstream from the waterfall. It 's steep downhill for the next 1.5 miles to the junction with Trail No. 216 near the South Fork of the Toutle River. You'll see standing dead trees that were singed by the blast along the route. If you follow Trail No. 216.9 across the river and up the steep barren hillside for 1.3 miles, Trail No. 216 G for 0.8 mile, and Castle Lake Trail No. 221 for 3.2 miles you'll arrive at the outlet end of the lake. This route is discussed more in Chapter 5.

(Road 81 discussion continued)-

At the junction of Road 8123 and Road 81, turn left and head toward Road 83. You'll cross the Blue Lake Horse Trail No. 237 after 0.5 mile. After another 0.2 mile you'll arrive at the former Kalama Springs Campground.

Kalama Springs

12 miles from SR 503
0.2 mile to the spring
Evidence of the alluvial flow that destroyed a campground

This is a unique feature for two reasons. In the late fall of 1980 heavy rain washed pumice from the upper slopes of the mountain, down the drainages, filling in flat areas, caves, and culverts and washing out roads. It buried this 16 unit campground with 3 foot deep silt, killing many of the trees and covering the tables.

The area was always unique because the Kalama River springs from under the lava flow here. People would come from Portland to fill water jugs with the pure spring water. Follow along the right hand fork of the pumice buried road for about 0.2 mile to the spring. You'll be surprised at the size of the river flowing from underneath the lava rock.

Red Rock Pass Trailhead for Toutle Trail No. 238

13.5 miles from SR 503
Elevation 3116 ft.

There's a small parking area that serves the traffic on the Toutle Trail and Butte Camp Area. It's used some for mountain climbing, and is discussed more in Chapter 5.

Road 8100830 to Climber's Bivouac

14.9 miles from SR 503
2.6 miles to Climber's Bivouac

This road is single-lane gravel and narrow with some steep side slopes, drive with extreme caution. The camping area is undeveloped and most camping occurs in the vehicles or in small tents. There is a comfortable compost type toilet. You'll need to bring your own drinking water as attempts to provide a well here have not been successful. It's 3765 feet in elevation and the best place to begin your climb of Mount St. Helens. The Ptarmigan Trail No. 216A provides trail access for the first 2 miles of the climb, and ties into the climbing route on Monitor Ridge.

Chapter 5

Upper Slopes

Timberline on Mount St. Helens is the lowest in the Cascade Range. The upper elevation for trees is around 6000 feet elevation at Mount Hood and Mount Adams, but here they disappear at around 4500 feet. Periodic volcanic activity over the past several thousand years has continually destroyed vegetation as it has attempted to advance up the slopes.

You'll enjoy the Loowit Trail No. 216 that completely in-circles the mountain at timberline. You can climb to the rim of the crater and look down at the steaming lava dome, and view Spirit Lake, Mount Rainier, Mount Hood, and Mount Adams. This chapter will provide you with some tips on the best way to enjoy this unique part of the Monument. The pumice is extremely fine and can be damaging to your camera lens and working parts. Protect it with a case and by keeping it in your pack.

For more detailed maps use USGS Quad E17.1

Loowit Trail No. 216

This 28 mile trail that completely in-circles the mountain at timberline is best described in segments since you will probably only use portions of it at one time. The type of use permitted also varies between some segments. The talcum-powder fine pumice could be damaging to the gear system on your bike.

Loowit Trail No. 216.1 (Trail No. 238.7 to Trail No. 240)

Most difficult, 2.2 miles
Hikers and mountain bikes
Elevation change from 3250 ft. to 4600 ft.

This portion of the trail is usually combined with the Sheep Canyon Trail No. 240, 2.3 miles, and segment 7 of the Toutle Trail No. 238, 1.5 miles, to make a loop for viewing the South Fork of the Toutle River. You'll see trees that were impacted by the blast and others that survived, as you're on the edge of the blast area. You'll want to go in on Trail No. 240 and down the steep Trail No. 216.1 to avoid a very steep climb in the other direction.

Loowit Trail No. 216.2 (Trail No. 240 to Trail No. 238A)

> **More difficult, 2.8 miles**
> **Hikers and mountain bikes**
> **Elevation change from 4600 ft. to 4780 ft.**

This is an excellent trail for experiencing the conditions at timberline. Hikers and mountain bikers will find it the least difficult portion of the entire trail around Mount St. Helens. You'll find it best to park a vehicle at both ends, and combine Trail No. 240 , 2.3 miles, Trail No. 216.2, 2.8 miles, Trail No. 238A, 2.7 miles, and Trail No. 238.3, 1.2 miles, for a total of about 9 miles.

If you're mountain biking you can park at either Sheep Canyon Trailhead on Road 8123 or Red Rock Pass on Road 81, and make a loop including the following trail segments: Trail No. 240, 2.3 miles, Trail No. 216.2, 2.8 miles, Trail No. 238A, 2.7 miles, and Trail No. 238.4, .5, and .6, 5.1 miles. You'll need to retrace either 0.7 mile of Trail No 240, or 1.2 miles of Trail No. 238.3 for a total of about 14 miles.

Loowit Trail No. 216.3 (Trail No. 238A to Trail No. 216A)

> **Most difficult, 2.5 miles**
> **Hikers and mountain bikes with extreme difficulty**
> **Elevation change from 4780 ft. to 4680 ft.**

Although this portion is open to mountain bikes, it is extremely difficult because the trail crosses the Swift Creek Lava Flow. There is no tread through this area and your bike will have to be carried for at least 0.5 mile. You can expect the trail tread to washout at most of the drainage crossings requiring more carrying of the bike.

You will probably use this segment with Trail No. 238.3, 1.2 miles, Trail No. 238A, 2.7 miles, and Trail No. 216A, 2.1 miles, to make a semi-loop from Red Rock Pass on Road 81 to Climber's Bivouac on Road 8100830. This is an 8.5 mile experience.

Loowit Trail No. 216.4 (Trail No. 216A to Trail No. 216B)

Most difficult, 3.1 miles
Hikers and mountain bikes
Elevation change from 4680 ft. to 3400 ft.

This segment is also open to mountain bikes, but you should be warned that the trail tread is not suitable for bikes over about half of its length. It crosses several lava fields, and the drainage's also washout annually.

It is usually traveled as a semi-loop from Climber's Bivouac on Road 8100830 to June Lake Trailhead on Road 83. This combines Trail No. 216A, 2.1 miles, Trail No. 216.4, 3.1 miles, and Trail No. 216B, 1.6 miles, for a nice day hike of 6.8 miles. The trail crosses near the top of a waterfall on Swift Creek that runs chocolate brown with silt. The only potential drinking water on the mountain is at Short Creek just a few hundred feet below Trail No. 216 on Trail No. 216B. The water flows out of the lava rock for a short distance and then disappears back into the lava. It is not shown on the quad maps.

Loowit Trail No. 216.5 (Trail No. 216B to Trail No. 234)

Most difficult, 5.0 miles
Hikers and mountain bikes, but not passable for bikes
Elevation change from 3400 ft. to 4140 ft.

This is an extremely difficult segment of the trail because of the deep drainage's that must be crossed. It almost requires climbing skills. It will depend on what condition the early summer snow melt has left the trail in at Pine Creek, Shoestring Creek and the Muddy River.

It is not a good place to take a bike. The unstable river channels will require climbing extremely steep banks. It is a beautiful area with views of Mount Adams and Mount Hood, and the extensive mudflow evidence in the Muddy River and Pine Creek.

This segment is best combined with the June Lake Trail No. 216B, 1.6 miles, and the Ape Canyon Trail No. 234, 5.5 miles, to make an 11 mile semi-loop requiring a drop-off or extra vehicle.

Loowit Trail No. 216.6 (Trail No. 234 to Trail No. 216D)

Top choice for mountain biking

More difficult, 1.8 miles
Hikers and mountain bikes
Elevation change from 4140 ft. to 4460 ft.

The trail begins at Ape Canyon on the south end and passes through the Plains of Abraham before intersecting with Abraham Trail No. 216D at the north end of the plain.

Ape Canyon Creek at one time flowed to the south and was blocked by a lava flow and spilled eastward across a low spot in the ridge. The load of sand and gravel carried by the creek has cut through the bedrock like a course file forming Ape Canyon within the last few centuries.

The canyon was named because of Ape-like creatures that allegedly attacked six men working their mine in this area. The miners returned to their homes in Longview with a report of apemen showering their cabin with large boulders one night in 1924. They reported encountering some of the apemen the next day. One of the creatures was believed slain and the body rolled into a deep ravine. Ape Canyon is believed to be that ravine.

The Plains of Abraham were swept clean of the small trees and large boulders that gave the inspiration for it's name by a mudflow from the melting glaciers directly above here. In time, small trees will re-colonize the area and more boulders will tumble down the steep slopes recreating a landscape similar to the pre-1980 condition.

This trail is best traveled by parking a vehicle at Ape Canyon Trailhead on Road 83 and being dropped-off at Windy Ridge Viewpoint. You take Truman Trail No. 207 for 1.8 miles, Abraham Trail No. 216D for 2.0 miles, and Ape Canyon Trail No. 234 for 5.5 miles. This gives you an 11 mile experience, mostly downhill. These connecting trails are discussed in Chapter 3.

Loowit Trail No. 216.7 (Trail No. 216D to Trail No. 216E)

More difficult, 2.0 miles
Hikers only
Elevation change from 4320 ft. to 4885 ft.

The trail climbs steeply for about one mile to Windy Pass, elevation 4885 feet. Mount Hood is visible at about 60 miles to the south and Mount Adams at about 30 miles to the east. The trail descends steeply for about one mile to a junction with Trail No. 216E. You can have an interesting 8.6 miles loop hike by parking at Windy Ridge and combining Truman Trail No. 207 for 2 miles, Trail No. 216E for 0.8 mile, Abraham Trail No. 216D for 2 miles and another !.8 miles of Truman Trail No. 207 with this 2 mile segment. It's ok to take your mountain bike to Windy Pass from the east end of this trail.

Loowit Trail No. 216.8 (Trail No. 216E to Trail No. 216G)

Most difficult, 7.8 miles
Hikers only
Elevation change from 4000 ft. to 4560 ft.

The first 1.3 miles of this trail provides access to an excellent view of the steaming-hot Loowit waterfall that flows out of the crater. This portion of the trail, combined with the first 2 miles of Truman Trail No. 207, 0.8 mile of No. Trail 216E and !000 feet. of Trail

No. 216F, provides a great experience on the debris avalanche and crater.

The trail becomes extremely difficult west of Loowit Falls. The steep draws are in a rapid period of change and you'll have some real challenges getting down the steep slopes and climbing back out. You can count on the trail being washed out at most of these crossings. This trail segment passes through some of the highest potential research areas in the Monument, and you are required to stay on the trail to prevent impact on the natural processes. The trail between Loowit Falls and the west end at the Castle Ridge Trail No. 216G is recommended only for very experienced backpackers and climbers.

Loowit Trail No. 216.9 (Trail No. 216G to Trail No. 238.7)

Most difficult, 1.3 miles
Hikers only
Elevation change from 4000 ft. to 3250 ft.

This portion of the trail descends steeply into the South Fork of the Toutle River Canyon and junctions with Toutle Trail No. 238.7 on the south side of the river. You can access this trail by driving to the Sheep Canyon Trailhead on Road 8123 and hiking Trail No. 240 for 0.7 mile and Trail No. 238.7 for 1.5 miles. You can also hike the Castle Ridge Trail No. 216G west for 2 miles to Weyerhaeuser Road 3000 and drive west to Castle Rock at Interstate 5. The maze of roads in this area are difficult to describe. If you plan to use them pick up a Weyerhaeuser St. Helens Tree Farm Map at one of the visitor centers.

Castle Lake Trail No. 221

More difficult, 3.2 miles
Hikers only
Elevation change from 4280 ft. to 2510 ft.

Segment 7 of the Loowit Trail No. 216 is an important link for those wanting to hike to **Castle Lake,** about 4 miles to the north. You would take

Trail No. 216G for 0.8 mile and the Castle Lake Trail No. 221 for 3.2 miles. The view of the debris avalanche in the North Fork of the Toutle River is worth the hike. If you're into fishing, Castle Lake, a 72 acre lake created by the avalanche, is said to have some 5 pound trout. Check the Washington State Fishing Regulations for season and special restrictions.

Mountain Climbing

One of the most exciting and memorable experiences that you can have is to climb Mount St. Helens. The views of the crater and dome are awesome from the rim of the crater. The new summit is at 8365 feet and you can drive to 3740 feet to begin your foot access, making it a climb that most physically fit people can handle.

The slopes of the mountain are covered with pumice that easily moves under foot traffic and daily use is limited, when the mountain is snow-free, to 100 climbers per day to protect the fragile slopes. The Forest Service is monitoring the mountain slopes to determine if this number of climbers per day is causing unacceptable change. We all need to search for solid footing and to pack out everything.

Permits

A permit is required for any access above the 4800 foot elevation level between May 15 and October 31. This is immediately above the Loowit Trail No. 216. During the remainder of the year climbers just simply register before and sign out after their climb at the register at Jack's Resaurant, 23 miles east of Woodland on SR 503.

Advanced reservations are available by mail or in person at the Mount St. Helens National Volcanic Monument Headquarters. Requests for reservations may be made after February 1. An early request increases your chance of reserving the date of your choice. Applications are considered in order of the postmark date or personal delivery date.

Within two weeks of receiving your application, the Forest Service will mail you a response. If your request dates are available, you will receive a permit and an information flyer. If none of the dates are available, you will be encouraged to apply again. There's probably a greater chance to achieve your date if it's a weekday.

Unreserved permits are assigned daily on a first-come, first-served basis at Jack's Restaurant located on SR 503, 23 miles east of Woodland. At 11:00 a.m. each morning a roster is made available for those wanting to climb the next day. Then, at 6:00 p.m. the names on the list are called in order, and permits are issued until the limit of 40 persons is reached. One person may represent up to a maximum party size of 12 people. You must be present at the 6:00 p.m. permit issuance to receive a permit. Name placement on the roster holds a spot in line, but does not guarantee a permit.

Each permit is valid for 24 hours, starting at midnight for the day of issue. Most climbers begin their ascent in the early morning to avoid the afternoon heat. Plan on taking at least 6 hours to reach the rim of the crater.

Volcanic Hazards

Mount St. Helens is an active volcano. Although the USGS can predict most eruptive activity days or weeks in advance, there is always some activity that is not predictable. The closer you get to the crater the more likely you could be surprised. Access into the crater is prohibited except for those monitoring the volcanic activity.

In case of eruptive activity, descend the mountain immediately. Avoid drainages which could channel mudflows. If there is an ash-fall, breath through a moist cloth, protect your eyes and descend into the wind. If the dome explodes, protect your head from falling rocks by hiding under or behind large boulders or cliffs.

The current volcanic advisory will be posted at the climber's register at Jack's Restaurant and will include the volcanic hazard level. The three levels of volcanic hazard are defined as follows:

Low Volcanic Hazard

The volcano is at or below normal background levels of volcanic activity. There is little chance that any eruptive activity will occur which would pose danger to persons outside the crater. The mountain is open to climbing.

Moderate Volcanic Hazard

The volcano is undergoing some activity that may lead to an eruption, (earthquakes, gas emissions, etc.). This level of unrest means there is a low to moderate level of danger to climbers outside the crater. Climbers should use caution and avoid a prolonged stay on the mountain.

High Volcanic Hazard

The volcano is undergoing major volcanic activity or is exhibiting unpredictable behavior. Hazardous eruptive activity is likely to develop soon or may be in progress. The mountain is closed to climbing until the hazard abates.

Climbing Safety

Even though the 8365 foot Mount St. Helens is not considered a difficult climb by experienced climbers, it's high elevation, irregular and frequently snow covered slopes and rapidly changing weather conditions can prove dangerous. For your enjoyment and safety you should have the following equipment.

- **Layered clothing** so you can regulate body temperature as the conditions change throughout the day.
- **Wind breaker** to protect you from chilling winds that are common at this elevation.
- **Rain gear** to keep you dry when the unexpected storm moves in.
- **Sunglasses** to protect you from the sun reflecting off the snow.
- **Glasses** in lieu of contact lenses as blowing ash can cause major eye discomfort.

- **Sunscreen** to protect you from the more intense ultraviolet rays at these high elevations.
- **Good hiking or climbing boots** to give you adequate ankle support on these steep side slopes.
- **Ice ax** to help keep you on the slope and to help you stop yourself if you begin to slide.
- **Crampons** to help you prevent sliding on steep snow and ice fields.
- **Food** to provide energy, especially if you get lost or injured and have to spent a night.
- **Drinking water,** as all routes are dry in the summer.
- **First aid kit** to take care of cuts and blisters.

Always climb with at least four people in your group. If someone becomes disabled and you need to go for help, leave one person with the injured party and send two for help. This ensures that no one is left alone.

Weather is the biggest hazard. It can be warm and sunny one minute and snowing the next. Visibility can suddenly be less than 50 feet. If you see a storm approaching, turn around and start your descent before you find yourself unable to see.

During winter and early spring, be alert to the potential for snow avalanches on lee and sun facing slopes. The crater rim is highly unstable. When on the rim, be careful not to cause additional rock fall or avalanche release as scientists may be working in the crater. Large and dangerous cornices of snow and ice often form on the rim. If you walk on these cornices they may break off and take you for a long fall into the crater.

For emergency assistance, use the telephones found at the following locations: Climber's Bivouac, Marble Mountain Sno-Park and at Pine Creek Information Station. These telephones automatically dial the Emergency Dispatch Center.

Mountain climbers enjoying the view from the rim of the crater. (Forest Service Photo)

Climbing Routes

Monitor Ridge

This is the primary route used by climbers during the summer. It has the easiest access and highest elevation of any of the possible starting points. It is reached by following Road 81 for about 15 miles to Road 8100830. Then drive north on Road 8100830 for 2.6 miles to Climber's Bivouac which is at the elevation of 3765 feet. The rim of the crater is only about 4.5 miles. The first two miles are on Ptarmigan Trail No. 216A.

Climber's Bivouac

22 miles from Jack's Restaurant on SR 503
Tent camping, no water
Composting toilet and emergency telephone

Most climbers begin their ascent from this trailhead camping area. Register at Jack's the evening before the climb and plan to begin your climb here early in the morning. There are no developed campsites but you can set up a small tent next to your vehicle or sleep in your pickup camper. Road 8100830 is a single-lane, gravel surfaced road that is moderately steep and you'll want to be experienced driving on this type of road before towing a trailer.

The snow melts from the road, permitting vehicle access, about the middle of June. You'll need to call the Monument Headquarters to determine accessibility. Bring drinking water for both camping and climbing.

Ptarmigan Trail No. 216A (Climber's Bivouac to Monitor Ridge)

Most difficult, 2.1 mile
Hikers and mountain bikes
Elevation change from 3765 ft. to 4680 ft.

In addition to providing trail access for mountain climbing, this trail provides access to the Loowit Trail No. 216 for hikers and mountain bikes. It is steep and the segments of Trail No. 216 accessed by it are impassable for mountain bikes. It is open, but I do not recommend you take your bike unless you like to carry it for long distances over lava rock. You're also likely to encounter some of the 100 climbers using the trail daily.

This trail is maintained by the Ptarmigan Mountaineering Club from Vancouver, WA. The trail was named for an artic bird seen on the south slopes of Mount St. Helens prior to the 1980 eruptions. This is the southern most portion of this birds range.

The trail passes through a noble fir forest and breaks out into a massive lava flow at the upper end. The Monitor Ridge climbing route is easily followed from here for about 2.5 miles to the rim of the crater. It is marked with wooden posts and blue wands. The first part of the climbing route crosses a series of lava flows which are steep and unstable boulder fields. The final 1000 feet below the summit is loose and erodible volcanic ash. The route is snow covered through early June, and generally free of snow by mid-July.

Butte Camp

This is a good choice if you want to backpack and camp near timberline. There is a meadow and year-round creek at 4033 feet elevation. It's about 5.5 miles to the summit from the trailhead at Red Rock Pass on Road 81. The first 4 miles are on maintained trails, No. 238.3 and No. 238A.

Butte Camp Trail No. 238A (Trail No. 238 to Trail No. 216)

More difficult, 2.7 miles
Hikers and mountain bikes
Elevation change from 3520 ft. to 4780 ft.

This trail is accessed from the trailhead at Red Rock Pass on Road 81 by 1.2 miles of Toutle Trail No. 238.3. The trailhead is at 3116 feet elevation, so there is an elevation gain to 4780 feet at the end of Trail No. 238A where it junctions with Trail No. 216. The recommended camping area is at Lower Butte Camp about 1.3 miles in from the beginning of Trail No. 238A or 2.5 miles from the trailhead. About 0.5 mile farther you'll find Upper Butte Camp at 4600 feet elevation This area is closed to camping to protect research that has been on-going here since 1980. This trail, when combined with Trail No. 216.2, Trail No. 240, and Trail No. 238, provides an interesting loop of about 15 miles for hiking or mountain biking.

The wide open slopes above Trail No. 216 provide an excellent climbing route while the slope is covered with snow. It provides excellent opportunities for glissading or skiing downhill. After the snow melts in June, the steep approach and unconsolidated volcanic ash transform the route into a very difficult climb.

Worm Flows

This is the primary winter route. You'll drive to the Marble Mountain Sno-Park on Road 83 about 18.6 miles from Jack's Restaurant. The snow is plowed to provide winter access for recreation with funding from the WA State Department of Recreation. You must have a Washington State Sno-Park permit to park here. The permits cost about $20.00 per season and are available at Jack's Restaurant and other businesses in Cougar. Three and seven day permits are also available.

Leave the Sno-Park at the west side of the parking area on Swift Creek Ski Trail No. 244B and proceed northward and join Trail No. 244. After about 2.5 miles you'll be above timberline. It's best to cross to the west side of Swift Creek, immediately upstream from Chocolate Falls. Proceed north along the first ridge system west of Swift Creek. This portion of the route ascends a series of lava flows, each a few hundred feet high. At about 7500 feet in elevation you'll join the Monitor Ridge route.

There is a warming hut at the Sno-Park, but it is strictly for dayuse. There is also a compost toilet and emergency telephone.

Scientific Equipment

The Geological Survey has monitoring equipment on the slopes of the mountain. You'll encounter antennas, glass reflectors, fence posts, wooden targets, steel rods and large steel tripods for holding survey equipment. This equipment is extremely sensitive. Please do not remove or in any way disturb it.

Mount St. Helens Trivia

John Dryer, first editor of the Portland, OR newspaper, The Oregonian, was in the first party that climbed Mount St. Helens in 1853. Mount St. Helens has become the second most climbed mountain in the world. Mount Fuji, Japan is the most climbed.

Muddy River Lahar

Over a decade after the 1980 eruption, new plant life is easy to find on the area that was wiped clean by the mudflow.

Lava Canyon Trail

This extraordinary trail provides experiences for all skill levels. The first half mile is a more difficult barrier-free trail. The next half mile is more difficult for hikers. The lower two miles is most difficult.

The Ladder

A young family carefully descends a thirty-foot steel ladder to discover the lower portion of Lava Canyon.

Harmony Falls

The scenery in the photograph below, taken from the deck of the Harmony Falls Lodge in 1976, provides sharp contrast to the landscape captured in the photograph on the facing page. The post eruption photo was taken in 1991 from about 300 feet directly above the old lodge location which is now covered by 200 feet of water.

Although it's over a mile downhill to the shoreline of Spirit Lake, the opportunity to view the floating trees up close and to look across Spirit Lake into the crater and dome makes the hike worth it all. Compare these two scenes and try to comprehend the event that occurred on May 18, 1980, when the top 1300 feet of the mountain slid away.

Lewis River Falls

Spectacular waterfalls like Lower Falls shown below and Upper Falls shown on the facing page are what qualified the North Fork of the Lewis River for nomination as a National Scenic River under the Wild and Scenic Rivers Act. Lower Falls Campground is located within easy walking distance from these falls. A short barrier-free trail provides wheelchair access to a viewpoint of the falls.

Upper Falls

Three major waterfalls within two miles make the portion of the Lewis River Trail between Lower Falls Campground and Upper Falls one of the most exciting trails in the Nation. Open to hikers, horses, llamas and mountain bikes this trail is enjoyed by many users.

Johnston Ridge

A short distance from the proposed observatory on Johnston Ridge the landslide material from Mount St. Helens overtopped the ridge creating a scene that you would expect to find in the dessert. Boundary Trail No. 1 and Truman Trail No. 207 will route hikers across this interesting feature.

Coldwater Peak

The trail to Coldwater Peak provides views directly into the crater. It's about 10 miles each way from Road 26 across Mt. Margaret Ridge on the Boundary Trail No.1 and is one of the most scenic hiking or mountain biking opportunities.

Ape Cave

The author in the lower passage of Ape Cave, the longest unitary lava tube in the continental United States. Guided tours are sometimes available in this portion of the lava tube. Call the Monument Headquarters for the schedule.

photo by Tom Iraci, Forest Service

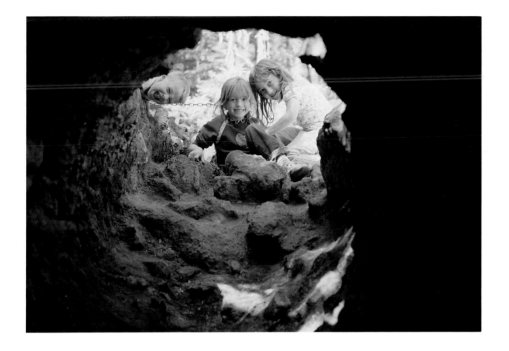

Tree Molds

About one mile from Ape Cave, The Trail of Two Forests Interpretive Trail explains how tree molds were created when lava flowed through an old-growth forest about 1800 years ago. These young girls are excited by the opportunity to crawl through a horizontal mold of a log. A barrier-free board- walk allows access for everyone while protecting the plants struggling for survival on the lava rock and keeping visitors from falling into deep vertical tree molds.

Ghost Lake

Many small lakes in the backcountry were impacted by the blast and ash fall. Ghost lake and Meta Lake are two lakes that are within easy hiking distance. The lakes are recovering much faster than first anticipated and fishing is permitted in some lakes. Check the Washington State Fishing Regulations to determine where fishing is allowed. Some lakes are being studied to observe the natural recovery process.

Blue Lake Horse Trail

Horse riding was very popular in the area around Mount St. Helens before the 1980 eruptions. Most of the area that was directly impacted by the blast has been closed to horse use to reduce the potential for introducing exotic plants from seeds passing through the horses digestive system. The introduction of these plants would impact the study of the natural processes. The Forest Service with volunteer assistance from organized horse groups has provided new trails for horse and llama users.

Winter Fun

Cross-country skier moves along smoothly on Road 83 which is groomed most of the winter. June Lake Trail No. 216B takes off from here toward Mount St. Helens for skiing only. The grooming is accomplished with funding from snowmobile licensing supplied to the Forest Service from the State. Cooperation between skiers and snowmobilers in planning for this area has resulted in improved trails, parking and support facilities.

Coldwater Ridge Visitor Center

The opening of the new Spirit Lake Memorial Highway, SR 504, to Coldwater Ridge in 1993 significantly changed the opportunities for discovery. Now, visitors can drive to the best viewpoints of Mount St. Helens in less than half a day.

photo by Frank Miller, Forest Service

Looking into the Future

What we see today as the portion of Mount St. Helens above timberline has been created in the last 2500 years. It has been active in the recent past and will continue to change. The only question is when and what kind of eruptive activity will occur next. Someday the crater will probably be filled again and the new mountain may be bigger than in the past. It may take 100 years, 2500 years or even longer. Hopefully, some more activity will occur in our lifetime so we can continue to discover the creative processes at work here.

Chapter 6

Road 26, Green River, Vanson Peak Backcountry

Road 26

About 9 miles south of Randle on Road 25 you'll find Road 26 going off to the west. Although this road is paved, it is very narrow and difficult to drive. It is used by many of the locals to gain quick access to Ryan Lake, Quartz Creek Big Trees, and trails leading to the Green River and Vanson Peak Backcountry. It also allows an interesting loop drive in combination with Roads 25 and 99. It's total length from the Miner's Car Interpretive Site on Road 99 to Road 25 is 17 miles.

> **For more detailed maps use USGS Quads D17.1, D17.2, D17.3 and D17.4.**

Quartz Creek Big Trees Trail No. 219

> **14 miles south of Randle**
> **Barrier-free, 0.6 mile Interpretive trail**
> **Hikers only**
> **Toilets, bus parking and turn around**
> **Elevation 1850 ft.**

At 13 miles south of Randle take Road 2608 east for about one mile to the parking area. This is an excellent example of old-growth Douglas-fir that survived the forest fires that changed the surrounding area. Some of the firs and cedars must be over 30 feet in circumference. Interpretive signs help us understand the natural processes that created this stand of timber and the habitat that it provides for different wildlife. It's a good place to bring your family or school class as the trail is easy and the messages clear.

It's accessible most of the year because of the low elevation. The hardwoods in the understory provide excellent color in the fall.

> *The barrier-free trail is rated more difficult for wheelchairs because of the grade and narrow clearing width. The toilets are barrier-free.*

Ryan Lake Viewpoint

19 miles from Randle
Easy, 0.6 mile Ryan Lake Interpretive Trail No. 222
Hikers only
Allow a minimum of 30 minutes
Interpretive signs, picnicking and toilets

This small lake near the edge of the lateral blast, about 12 miles from the crater, was the scene of a grim event on May 18, 1980. Ron Conner was camped on the north side of the lake. His van was parked in the small turnout along Road 2612. The blast blew timber down in all directions, covering the small campground and toilets. His body was found behind one of the toilet buildings buried under several inches of ash and other debris.

A pickup truck with a horse trailer was found just west of the van. It belonged to two men who had planned to ride the Goat Mountain Trail No. 217 to Deadman's Lake. The trail was blocked by snow and they apparently rode their horses about 2 miles west on Road 2612 and camped at Polar Star Mine. One of the men was found dead in his sleeping bag. The other had survived the blast and walked back to the truck. This must have been an extremely difficult task since the road was blocked by hundreds of toppled trees. Upon reaching the truck he apparently drank a beer as an empty can was found on top of the ash on the truck. His body was found by search dogs 5.2 miles from the truck on Road 26 under an ash-covered sleeping bag.

A 0.6 mile interpretive trail tells about the salvage of the blown-down timber in this area and the replanting by the Forest Service. The trail is hiker only but is not barrier-free.

The toilets, picnic tables and interpretive signs are barrier-free.

Green River, Vanson Peak Backcountry

Prior to the eruptions in 1980, the Mt. Margaret Backcountry Area north of Spirit Lake was one of the most popular horse packing and backpacking areas in the state. This area was impacted by the lateral blast and scientists are extremely interested in studying the recovery of the many small lakes. Trails are planned into the area but are delayed until a detailed analysis is completed.

Pack animals will not be allowed into the lakes area, and overnight camping may be regulated to protect the lake shore vegetation.

The Forest Service has attempted to replace some of the opportunities for pack animals that were lost by improving and increasing trail opportunities in the backcountry north of the Green River.

Goat Mountain Trail No. 217

More difficult, 8.6 miles
Hikers, mountain bikes, horses and llamas
Elevation change from 3400 ft. to 5100 ft.

The trailhead is 0.4 mile west of the junction of Roads 26 and 2612 along Road 2612. The trail begins in an area that was salvage logged following the blast and quickly enters into a lush green forest of moss draped Douglas-firs. It is cruelly steep for the first 2 miles, and continues to climb for about 5 miles to the top of the ridge at about 4600 feet elevation. You are rewarded by wildflowers, huckleberries and excellent views of the Green River Valley, Mount Rainier, Mount Adams, and Mount St. Helens.

At about 5.5 miles from the road you'll come upon Deadman's Lake an excellent place to camp and fish. **Trail 217D** takes you about 0.2 mile to the best camping. The trees around the lake survived the blast but you'll see how new pumice covers the lake bottom.

A short distance past Deadman's Lake you'll see the **Tumwater Mt. Trail No. 218** leading off to the north. This trail provides access into Goat Creek and a new trailhead on Forest Service Road No. 2750 on the west edge of the Monument. In combination with **Goat Creek Trail No. 205,** it ties back into this trail near Vanson Peak to provide a 14.5 mile loop opportunity.

From the junction with Trail No. 218 the main trail continues along the ridge providing more excellent views. At about 7 miles the **Goat Creek Trail No. 205** and **Vanson Peak Trail No. 217A** both take off in a northerly direction. Trail No. 217A is a loop trail of 1.25 miles that provides access to Vanson Peak. It's about 0.7 mile uphill to Vanson Peak, at an elevation of 4948 feet. There are dramatic views of the surrounding forest. The foundation of the former fire lookout building is still visible. Goat Creek Trail No. 205 will be described separately.

Approximately 7.5 miles on the main Trail No. 217 from Road 26 you'll come to the **Vanson Lake Trail No. 217B** to the left. This 0.3 mile trail takes you down hill to an excellent campsite and the lakeshore. It's a beautiful lake that reflects the surrounding forest when the wind and light are right.

Approximately 0.1 mile farther on the main Trail No. 217, at about 7.6 miles from Road 26, you'll find **Vanson Ridge Trail No. 213A.** It provides a 3.3 mile connection to the **Green River Trail No. 213**. This allows a nice 17 mile loop opportunity.

If you continue on for about 1.0 mile on the main Trail 217 you'll come to private Road 2750. The shortest trail access to Vanson Peak and the lake would be from this trailhead. The maze of roads are difficult to follow and could be closed at the discretion of the land owner. The trailhead is at the section corner common to sections 21, 22, 26, and 27 of T.11N., R.5E.

Sometimes these private access roads are closed because of high fire danger. You should call the Randle Ranger Station, (206) 497-7565, to check on the road status before leaving home.

Vanson Ridge Trail No. 213A

More difficult, 3.3 miles **Hikers, mountain bikes,horses and llamas** **Elevation change from 4600 ft. to 2360 ft.**

This trail provides a loop opportunity by linking the Goat Mt. Trail No. 217 to the Green River Trail No. 213. If you make the loop you will have to walk or ride on the 4 miles of road between the Green River Trailhead and the Goat Mt. Trailhead, or park a vehicle at both places. The loop provides an interesting and challenging 16 miles of trail.

Trail No. 213A takes you along some cliffs that provide dramatic views of the Green River. You'll see some of the biggest old-growth Douglas-fir trees remaining on the Gifford Pinchot National Forest where this trail joins the Green River Trail.

Green River Trail No. 213

More difficult, 7.5 miles **Hikers, mountain bikes, horses llamas** **Elevation Change from 2560 ft. to 1880 ft.**

This trail begins at a trailhead on Forest Service Road 2612036 about 3.75 miles from the junction of Roads 26 and 2612.

The trail follows downstream along the Green River for 7.5 miles to the Weyerhaeuser Co. Road 2500. This road is accessed from the small town of Kid Valley on SR 504, about 20 miles east of I-5. It's generally open for recreational use, but if fire danger is high you better check with Weyerhaeuser Co. in Longview before beginning your trip. Because of the low elevation the trail is snow-free very early in the year and makes a good spring opportunity.

At the Road 2612 end of the trail you'll be in blown-down trees for the first 0.5 mile. After about 2 miles you'll be in some very large old-growth Douglas-fir. This is prime habitat for spotted owls. At about 5 miles you'll come to the junction with the Vanson Ridge Trail No. 213A. If you want to make a 16 mile loop, returning via the ridge, take this trail to the north. If you continue down stream, after about 0.5 mile, hike over to the river and see the main waterfall on the Green River. If you continue to the end of the trail, the trailhead is at the site of an old ranger station that served this area about 1920.

There is evidence of former mining activity and the Minnie Lee Mine is signed about 2 miles in from the Ryan Lake end. There are many good opportunities for camping and fishing along the trail.

Tumwater Trail No. 218

More difficult, 9 miles
Hikers, mountain bikes, horses and llamas
Elevation change from 4600 ft. to 2400 ft.

This trail takes off the Goat Mt. Trail No. 217 near Deadman's Lake about 5.5 miles from Road 2612. The trail is on Tumwater Ridge for the first 5 miles as it goes in a northerly direction. There are beautiful views of Mount Adams, Mount Rainier, and Strawberry Mt. Tumwater Peak Spur Trail No. 218A takes off at about 5 miles and goes 0.2 mile to the peak. You are rewarded with excellent views in all directions.

A little farther along the trail you skirt a small dry lake bed that has become a meadow and a popular place for elk. Keep quiet and look closely and you may see some interesting wildlife. The trail begins to descend into Goat Creek beyond the meadow. There is a 2000 foot elevation change in the next 4 miles. The trail junctions with the Goat Creek Trail No. 205 at the confluence of Goat Creek and it's west fork.

Goat Creek Trail No. 205

Best choice for a short hike to a waterfall

More difficult, 6 miles
Hikers, mountain bikes, horses and llamas
Elevation change from 2200 ft. to 4600 ft.

This trail links Trail No. 217 with Trail No. 218 and also ties them into a trailhead on Forest Service Road No. 2750. The trailhead is accessed by turning south off US 12 on Cosmos Road, about 6 miles east of Morton. Almost immediately, you turn left onto private road No. 2700 and follow it for 5 miles to a bridge at the upper end of Riffe Reservoir. Proceed for about one mile and take Forest Service Road No. 2750 for about 3 miles to the trailhead near the end of the road.

Tacoma City Light Company is planning to build a campground near the bridge at the upper end of Riffe Lake. This will provide the best overnight camping opportunity for users of the Goat Creek and Vanson Peak trails.

If you want to see one of the most picturesque waterfalls on the Monument, hike the level first mile of this trail to Leona Falls. The trail goes into a grotto behind the falls for almost 300 feet. The water drops about 100 feet over a moss and fern covered cliff onto a rock dome and cascades for another 40 feet into Goat Creek.

At about 2 miles, the trail junctions with Tumwater Trail No. 218. The trail climbs steeply for the next 4 miles, skirting several meadows, before it joins the Goat Mt. Trail No. 217 near Trail No. 217A junction. It provides several loop opportunities. The best is the 19 miles possible by combining Trails No. 205, Trail No. 217 and Trail No. 218.

Occasionally, the private access is closed for fire danger. You should call the Randle Ranger Station, (206) 497-7565 to check on the road status before leaving home.

Boundary Trail No. 1 Norway Pass Trailhead

Best photo opportunities across Spirit Lake

25 miles from Randle via Road 26
30 miles from Randle via Road 99
Serves the Boundary Trail east and west
Water via a hand pump

This is my favorite trail. It's a steep climb for the first 2.2 miles to Norway Pass, but once you gain this elevation it's an easy hike across Mt. Margaret Ridge. You should at least go an additional 3 miles to the viewpoint at Mt.

Margaret. You can view the lakes area of the backcountry and see the classic view of Mount St. Helens across Spirit Lake.

If you can spent a long day, try hiking or mountain biking the full 9 miles to Coldwater Peak Trail No. 1F. It's a steep 0.6 mile to the old lookout site. You'll be rewarded with outstanding views of Mount St. Helens, Mount. Rainier, and St. Helens Lake. Then hike another 0.8 mile down Trail No. 1 to the natural rock arch. It's a wonderful photo opportunity as you look one way through the arch at Mount St. Helens and the other way at Mount. Adams. Trail No. 1, is open to hikers only beyond the Trail 1F, junction. This could change in the future, once the Forest Service can analyze the foot traffic on Trails No. 211, No. 230, and No. 230A. The long distance from the parking lot at Coldwater Lake may limit foot visitors.

If you're on foot, plan to hike 19 miles one way and come out at Windy Ridge. You'll need to have a full day and leave an extra vehicle at Windy Ridge. It is 12 miles from Norway Pass Trailhead to Truman Trail No. 207 on Trail No. 1. It is an additional 7 miles down the debris avalanche that over-topped Johnston Ridge, and across the Spirit Lake Basin to Windy Ridge on Trail No. 207. This is the most picturesque and exciting trail in the Monument. You need to be an experienced backpacker to complete this 19 miles in one day.

It's also an interesting trail experience if you go east from Norway Pass on Trail No. 1 to Ghost Lake. It's about 2 miles to the junction with the Ghost Lake Trail No. 1H. The lake is only 0.4 mile from Trail 1. From Road 26 the trail climbs to the top of the ridge through trees toppled by the blast. Next it passes through an area of white snags and drops into a basin forested with occasional islands of old-growth trees. Trail 1H takes off to the north across a large marsh and passes through a stand of green trees before entering an area of downed trees surrounding Ghost Lake. Plan this trip for August and enjoy the largest huckleberries on the forest. You'll also obtain a splendid view into the Green River Valley.

Chapter 7   Road 90, Lewis River

Lewis River Falls Area

One of the most scenic rivers in the country is in the vicinity of the Mount St. Helens National Monument. The North Fork of the Lewis River, which is proposed for designation as a Scenic River under the Wild & Scenic River Act, has numerous waterfalls that are accessible by roads or trails. The entire upper drainage area has been managed to retain its natural beauty.

The best access to this proposed Scenic River is to take Exit 21 on Interstate 5 at Woodland and drive east on SR 503. The Lewis River will be to your right for the next 48 miles. The lower portion of the river has been harnessed by three dams that generate power for the Northwest. These reservoirs provide recreational opportunities, and you may wish to camp in one of the Pacific Power & Light Company's campgrounds while visiting the Monument or Scenic River. There is good fishing at all three reservoirs.

The first good campground is at the upper end of Merwin Reservoir. You drive 23 miles to Jack's Restaurant and turn right toward Battle Ground on the main SR 503 for 5 miles to the Cresap Bay Campground. There is more on this campground in Chapter 10.

As you continue east on SR 503 Spur from Jack's toward Cougar, Yale Reservoir is on the right. It is popular for sailing because of the consistent winds. It is also known for good late summer fishing for Kokanee Salmon. If you're visiting the area in September, stop at Cougar Creek, about one mile east of Cougar, and look for the bright red spawning salmon in the creek. If you're here in summer, turn into the Cougar Picnic area and enjoy the nice swimming area. The two P P & L Campgrounds, Cougar and Beaver Bay are described in Chapter 10.

Just beyond the Beaver Bay Campground entrance, about 3.5 miles east of Cougar, the SR 503 Spur becomes Forest Service Road 90. On your left is a canal that was constructed by P P & L as a mitigation to Cowlitz County PUD since they had filed with the federal government first, for a power withdrawal. The canal is stocked with trout and is a good place to fish with children early in the season.

After climbing for about 4 miles you'll find an excellent overlook of the Swift Dam and Reservoir on the right side of the road. Swift Reservoir is one of the best trout fishing waters in Southwest Washington and a good portion of the fishing occurs from near the dam. About 0.1 mile farther there is a splendid view of Mount St. Helens. This was a much photographed view between March 27 and May 18, 1980, as it was one of the few safe places that the media was allowed access.

As you drive the next 12 miles along Swift Reservoir, you'll see evidence of massive amounts of logging. This is private land that was exploited because of an agreement that the railroad company made with a logging company to develop the roads into the area. This entitled the logging company to all the timber at a very low price. Unfortunately, the agreement had a termination date of 1999. This caused the accelerated timber harvest you see in this portion of the Lewis River. Fortunately, reforestation was required and this is an excellent tree growing area. In a few years it will be difficult to determine that the area was so aggressively logged.

The Forest Service manages land in Drift Creek on the south side of the reservoir, as old-growth habitat for species like eagles and spotted owls that are dependent on these conditions for survival. They also control the small area where the former ranger station is located.

Near the upper end of the reservoir you'll find the Swift Forest Camp, the Pine Creek Information Station and the Eagle Cliff Store. At the junction of Roads 90 and 25 you are 48 miles from Woodland. From this point upstream you are in the Scenic River corridor. You continue on Road 90 across the Eagle Cliff Bridge. The scenic area you are about to enter is beautiful any time of the year but I recommend that you go in May or early June when the water flow is high.

There are several recreational sites developed to provide barrier-free trail experiences in this river corridor making it an excellent full day trip or overnight for the physically challenged.

For more detailed maps for trails use USGS Quads E18.1, E18.2, E18.3

Curly Creek Falls Viewpoint

This is a very important trailhead for a barrier-free trail to viewpoints of waterfalls on Curly Creek and Miller Creek, and also for extended hikes and rides on the Lewis River Trail. Drive northeast for 4 miles on Road 90 from the Eagle Cliff Bridge and turn west onto Road 9039. This is a difficult turn because Road 9039 comes in at a 30 degree angle and it is a very sharp turn. Drive about 0.5 mile and cross the Lewis River, then continue uphill for about 0.2 mile. The Curly Creek Viewpoint is on the left. The trails are as follows:

Curly Creek Falls Trail No. 31A

Barrier-free easy trail, 800 feet
Hikers only
Elevation 1200 ft.

This short trail is constructed of compacted gravel to provide a more difficult wheelchair experience. It's a great trail for children and the physically challenged. The trail is closed to horses and mountain bikes as they would impact the gravel surface with ruts. Viewing platforms and handrails are provided at both waterfall sites. The jade green Lewis River, flowing through a bedrock channel 50 feet below, adds to the peaceful forest scene.

Curly Creek Falls on the opposite side of the Lewis River plunges 75 feet into the river. The power of the water has carved two rock arches that make this waterfall very unique. At the end of the trail you'll see Miller Creek fall about 75 feet into the river over a moss and fern covered cliff.

Lewis River Trail No. 31, Segment 1

More difficult, 11 miles
Hikers, mountain bikes, horses and llamas
Elevation change from 1260 ft. to 1800 ft.

This trail is one of the most popular early spring trails in the Gifford Pinchot National Forest. It is extremely popular with the mountain bikers since there is so little elevation change and you can ride back on the road to make a 20 mile loop. The trail is rated more difficult but with the exception of a steep grade at Cussed Hollow Creek it is easy. It's 9.5 miles from Curly Creek Viewpoint to the next road crossing which is just east of the bridge on the Lewis River near Crab Creek.

This trail provides peaceful access along the Lewis River through a cool and green forestland. It passes through magnificent groves of old-growth Douglas-fir and Western Red Cedar trees that survived the many fires that created the vast stands of young trees in the Lewis River area.

At about 3 miles is the historic Bolt Camp Shelter which was built in 1931. It was occupied for harvesting cedar shake bolts that were used in the construction of settlements downstream. The shelter was recently restored by Troop 349, Boy Scouts of America, and Amboy Horsemen. The shelter is open to you on a first-come, first-served basis for camping. During the week you'll probably find it empty. The shelter can sleep four on its rustic split cedar bunks.

The trail climbs to the top of the 300 foot high basalt cliffs that form Cascade Gorge about mid-way between Curly Creek and Road 90. There are some excellent views of the river from the edge of the cliffs.

At about 8.5 miles the trail gradually descends to the Lewis River. This is a good area for seeing springboard holes in some of the huge stumps. These were cut into the trees by loggers so they could stand on a board and be clear of brush and above the thicker portion of the tree trunk. Tree falling at that time was done with axes and cross-cut saws, and was hard physical work. The wood was selling for almost nothing and although it seems wasteful by today's standards, it probably made good sense to leave these high stumps 50 years ago.

The trail crosses Cussed Hollow Creek on a bridge and follows the river for about 1 mile to the Road 90 crossing. Crab Creek flows into the Lewis River from the east just upstream from the road bridge. This is a popular put-in place for experienced river rafters who float about 15 miles into Swift Reservoir. Floating seems to be most successful with inflatable kayaks and before the end of June.

This trail segment continues for 1.2 miles to the Lower Falls on the Lewis River which is one of the major attractions in this area. The falls are over 100 feet wide and fall 40 feet into a deep pool. The uniform cascade of water gives it the look of a miniature Niagara Falls. There is a campground nearby that provides excellent access to the falls and this end of the trail.

Bridle Path Trail No. 31B

Easy, 0.3 mile
Hikers, mountain bikes, horses and llamas
Elevation change from 1800 ft. to 1750 ft.

Across Road 9039 from the Curly Creek Viewpoint is the former trailhead for the Lewis River Trail. A 0.3 mile portion of trail is maintained from here to the Lewis River Trail to provide an alternate route for horses and mountain bikes. This helps to reduce congestion at the viewpoint parking and prevent damage to the barrier-free trail.

It also is a good location for overnight camping.

Lower Falls Campground

First choice for waterfalls photography

66 miles from Woodland
43 campsites for tents or RV's
Barrier-free trail to waterfall

About 1.5 miles north of the road bridge across the Lewis River you'll see the Lower Falls Campground entrance sign on the right side of the road. This is about 18 miles upriver from the Pine Creek Information Station or 66 miles from Woodland on I-5.

The Native Americans camped here while harvesting the salmon that bunched up below the 40 foot waterfall which was the first fish barrier on this river. The Forest service has provided a short barrier-free trail to the viewpoint of the falls. An interpretive sign explains the seasonal migration of the natives in search of, and harvesting of, food. The fishing is good today for trout. You'll need to bushwhack down to the pool. This is also the best place to set up your tripod and photograph the waterfall.

This was a popular campground with horse users before it was recently reconstructed and enlarged. A new horse camp is being constructed about 3 miles east off Road 93 near Quartz Creek. This is being done by local horse clubs with funding from the State of Washington Interagency Committee for Outdoor Recreation. It should be available for use in 1994.

There currently is no fee, but donations are accepted. This could change as use increases. Check with the Monument Headquarters or plan on paying about $7.00. The campground season is usually April through October.

The campground and day use area are barrier-free. The 300 foot barrier-free trail to the viewpoint and interpretive sign provide one of the Gifford Pinchot National Forest's best experiences for physically challenged visitors.

This is one of my favorite places to bring visitors, and once you try it you'll come back often with friends.

Lewis River Trail No. 31, Segment 2

Best scenery for miles traveled

Easiest, 3.25 miles
Hikers, mountain bikes, horses and llamas
Elevation change from 1800 ft to 2000 ft.

The day use area at Lower Falls also serves as a trailhead for the Lewis River Trail. The portion of this trail that goes north is an exciting segment of the trail that is carved out of steep hillside and sometimes cliffs. It's rated as an easy trail by the Forest Service, but it can be dangerous. Keep tight control of your children. If you're riding, dismount and walk your horse or mountain bike past the area where there are steep drop-offs.

A short distance north of the campground you'll see the remains of an old sheep bridge and steam donkey. The old piece of machinery is believed to have been used by the permittee to move the bridge in and out of place to avoid it's loss to the winter floods on the river. Sheep from southeast of Mount Adams were driven across the bridge to access grazing areas on Spencer Butte.

About 1 mile past the campground you'll cross Copper Creek on a bridge. You'll hear the roar of the Middle Falls on the Lewis River which is just a short distance up the trail. It's the smallest of the 3 major waterfalls on the river. It is more of a long cascade than the other two falls which drop for 40 feet each. You can walk down to the stream bank to get pictures of the falls and also the trail bridge. You may need your tripod as it's a heavy forest canopy with deep shadows.

Middle Falls Trail No. 31C joins the main Trail No. 31 about 0.25 mile south of Copper Creek and leaves it near the Middle Falls. This trail makes a loop opportunity of 0.75 mile to a trailhead on Road 90. There is a great view of Copper Creek Falls that is crossed by the trail bridge. It's open to hikers only and is a more difficult short hike that provides a lot of outstanding scenery.

The main trail continues up river and after another mile you'll see the Upper Falls. It's very similar to the Lower Falls, about 40 feet high and 100 feet wide. The falls form a horseshoe-shaped amphitheater that often produces a rainbow from the spray. There's a good photo spot along the trail just beyond Alec Creek. The best photos require getting into the river about 300 feet down stream. In the summertime you won't even need to get your feet wet.

The trail crosses Alec Creek on a wooden bridge and climbs along a cliff to the top of the falls. There is a 150 foot spur trail to the viewpoint at the top of the falls. A flat staging area with a hitching rail has been provided so you can leave your horses, llamas or mountain bikes while you hike to the viewpoint.

The main trail continues for about 1.2 miles to Road 90 at the confluence of Quartz Creek and the Lewis River. There is an exceptional grove of old-growth trees here that will give you new appreciation for the ancient forest. **Quartz Creek Trail No. 5** begins just across the road and follows Quartz Creek for about 10 miles where it ties into the Boundary Trail No. 1. This is an extremely difficult trail because of it's location and condition. Stream crossings are difficult for animals and bikes. It's scheduled for reconstruction in the next several years, and my recommendation is to delay using all but the first 2 miles of the Quartz Creek Trail until after the reconstruction.

Big Creek Falls Trail No. 28

Easy, 0.6 mile, barrier-free, 0.1 mile
Hikers and mountain bikes
Elevation change from 1920 ft. to 1800 ft.

About 9 miles north of Pine Creek Information Station you'll see the entrance sign for the Big Creek Trail No. 28. A couple of hundred feet, by barrier-free trail, from the small parking area you'll be rewarded with a magnificent view. This 110 foot waterfall is beautiful at any time of year. My favorite time is Fall, when the hardwoods growing on the cliffs are in their brilliant colors.

A viewing platform, that provides the "ultimate view", was constructed in 1992 by the Northwest Youth Corps. A secure railing allows easy and safe access to the cliff edge. Be especially attentive to children as there are cliffs in the area.

The old-growth Douglas-fir here are over 500 years old. Notice how many of these ancient trees are losing giant branches to the strong winter winds, or have dead tops from insects and diseases. The young trees you see at ground level are mostly hemlock as they can live in heavy shade. They may be 50 years old because of the slow growth that occurs in dense shade. The trees around the parking area are mostly Douglas-fir that were planted after logging about 1965. In the open sunlight caused by the timber cutting they will grow vigorously until they form a dense forest.

The trail continues as an easy hiking and mountain biking trail for another 0.6 mile to a panoramic view of the Lewis River drainage. It's amazing and rewarding to see so much forestland that appears to be undisturbed by humans. Across the Lewis River you can see Hemlock Falls free-falling to the canyon below.

The new viewing platform will allow you to obtain the ultimate view of this falls, the experience in the old-growth on this barrier-free trail of compacted gravel is worth your time and effort. Combining this experience with viewing the waterfalls at Curly Creek and Lower Falls can make for a very enjoyable full day.

Most difficult trails can be hard to follow since the tread may be invisible as on this mudflow on the upper slopes of Mount St. Helens.

Chapter 8   Winter Recreation

Every year more and more people come to Mount St. Helens in the winter time. It's beautiful with a new covering of pure white snow and provides a completely different experience. Two principle access routes are maintained throughout the winter with Sno-Park funding from the Washington State Parks and Recreation Commission. Forest Service Road 90 and Road 83 are open to Cougar and Marble Mountain Sno-Parks on the south side of the mountain. Forest Service Road 25 south from Randle is open to the Wakapish Sno-Park.

Sno-Parks

A Sno-Park permit is required to park in any of these snow-cleared areas and the funds collected are used to keep these parking areas open. Permits are available at Jack's Restaurant, the Cougar Store, Yale Lake Store and Eagle Cliff Store on the south. They are available at the Randle and Packwood Ranger Stations on weekdays, and at Blanton's Grocery in Packwood for recreationists planning to use the north side. They can also be obtained by writing to the Office of Winter Recreation, Washington State Parks Commission, 7150 Cleanwater Lane KY-11, Olympia , WA 98504 or calling (206) 754-1250.

In 1993 a seasonal permit cost $20.00, a one-day permit $7.00, and a three-day permit $10.00. The permits are good at all Sno-Parks in either Washington or Oregon. Vehicles licensed in Washington State must have the Washington State Sno-Park permit displayed on the windshield.

The State of Washington will be maintaining SR 504 to the visitor center at Coldwater Lake year-round. Although no trails have been marked, you can expect to see winter recreation begin to grow in the area around Elk Rock in the future. At the present time Sno-Park permits are not required at the end of SR 504.

Snow Conditions:

Snow on the west side of the Cascades is usually dense and wet and difficult to move around in. The dry powder we all dream about is rare and short lived because the normal freezing level is about 4000 feet. Trail grooming is provided on many of the roads in the area by funding through the Washington State Parks and Recreation Commission. This provides conditions that make skiing and snowmobiling feasible. Funding for the grooming comes from snowmobile license fees. Cross-country skiers get to use the groomed trails free and should remember to be friendly to the snowmobilers. Many of the ski trails were constructed to allow for grooming in the future. If you want the area groomed, make your desire known to the Winter Recreation Managers, Washington State Parks Commission, 7150 Cleanwater Lane, KY-11, Olympia, WA 98504 or call (206) 754-1250.

The weather conditions at Mount St. Helens can result in unstable slopes that are prone to avalanche. These usually occur beginning in mid-winter when the snow is deep and warming trends are frequent. The upper slopes of the mountain in the Plains of Abraham and Shoe String areas have high potential for avalanches. For current snow avalanche and weather forecasts call (503) 326-2400 for a 24 hour recorded message.

The trails marked with orange diamonds for snowmobiling and blue diamonds for cross-country skiing are in locations that are of very low avalanche hazard. There are wonderful viewing opportunities available by going off-trail. Check the weather and snow conditions before doing this to avoid getting caught in an avalanche.

Multiple Use Trails

The Mount St. Helens area is popular with all kinds of snow users. Prior to the eruption in 1980, most of the use on the south side of the mountain was by snowmobilers. Cross-country skiing use was growing very fast on the north side of the mountain around Spirit Lake. The eruption displaced these north side users. The Forest Service has worked closely with both the skiers and snowmobilers to try to replace the opportunities lost at Spirit Lake with new parking and trails to the south and east of the mountain.

All users are trying to co-exist together. They have worked together on planning the facilities and marking the trails. It is very important that all users practice the winter etiquette described in the next section. Conflicts will occur but are usually the result of errors in grooming, trail locations, or lack of signing. If you have a problem, make sure the Forest Service is informed.

The Oregon Nordic Club and the Vancouver Trail Riders are helping to maintain these trails as partners with the Gifford Pinchot National Forest.

Snowmobilers are requested to stay off of trails that are designated with only blue markers. All users must obey the administrative closures that are in affect to protect the research values and monitoring equipment. These include the Crater and Pumice Plain between the volcano and Spirit Lake. Snowmobiles cannot go beyond Windy Pass. The Goat Marsh Research Natural Area west of Road 8123 is closed to all vehicles.

Planning Your Winter Trip

A trip into the Mount St. Helens Monument in the winter will take a lot more preparation. The road will probably be covered with snow or ice, and you'll need to have the car ready. Make sure that the traction devices, chains, fit your car and are stored where you can easily find them. It is usually possible to get to the Sno-Park with good studded snow tires or 4-wheel drive. The chains are a good idea for that occasion when you get stuck. Always fill up the gas tank before heading into the forest.

Plan your clothing in layers so that you can remove or add garments as your body heats and cools. In the mountains, warmth is very crucial for safety, while style and flexibility are less important than at the more highly developed downhill ski areas. It's my experience that wool is the best. It will keep you warm even if it gets wet. Plan to protect yourself from the rain and snow by taking along rain gear. Rain pants and jackets made of coated nylon or breathable waterproof material are a good investment in your comfort. Always take along the ten essentials mentioned in the Introduction.

Pack food for a picnic lunch and bring along lots of snacks to carry on the trail. Bring lots to drink, both hot and cold, as the body dehydrates rapidly when expending energy in the snow.

Discuss your trip with a close relative or friend. Give them an estimated time that you'll return so that in the event you don't, a search and rescue operation can begin.

Winter Etiquette

Speedy snowmobilers and skiers should slow down when approaching other users on the trails. Step out of the way so the other users can easily pass.

Keep to the right when meeting others and yield the right-of-way to downhill traffic.

Park considerately. Try not to stop in the middle of the road to put on your chains. Take no more space in the parking lot than needed. Avoid blocking other vehicles or impeding access to the trails. Keep turn-around areas clear.

Leave your pets at home. There are hazards such as tree wells, avalanches, thin ice and cold streams that could harm them. Their toilet habits can cause discomfort for other trail users. They could be threatening to other users and wildlife.

Pack out everything you bring in and help the Forest Service by removing litter left behind by those less considerate.

Cougar and Marble Mountain Sno-Parks

From Woodland, at exit 21 on Interstate 5, take SR 503 for 28 miles east to the town of Cougar. Remember to pick up a Sno-Park permit, gas or food. Continue east for about 8 miles to Road 83. Turn left on Road 83 and continue for about 2 miles to Road 8303. If you want to ski to Ape Cave, turn left and park in the small parking area at the Trail of Two Forests. Continue on Road 83 for about 1 mile to the Cougar Sno-Park where Road

81 junctions with Road 83. If you want to play at Marble Mountain Sno-Park continue for about 3 miles straight ahead. You are about 42 miles from Woodland. In winter, plan on about 1 1/2 hours driving time each way.

Cougar Sno-Park

Parking for about 20 vehicles with trailers
Groomed trails, open to skiing and snowmobiling
Chemical toilets
Open December 20 to March 31

This Sno-Park serves the snow trails on the west side of the mountain. Other than the Goat Marsh Research Natural Area all trails are open to all users. The West Fork Snowmobile Trail is not recommended for skiers because of narrow width and blind curves. The most popular opportunities are as follows:

Trail No. 8100 (Sno-Park to Kalama Horse Camp)

Groomed, 15 miles round trip, easy

It was the plan to someday remove snow from Road 81 from SR 503 Spur to the Kalama Horse Camp, and use it for a separate Sno-Park for cross-country skiing. This would allow those skiers searching for solitude the opportunity to distance themselves from snowmobilers. This plan seems to have been lost to the reality of cost. If skiers still feel they need this opportunity they need to keep the Forest Service informed.

The area is generally level and suitable for skiing. The Goat Marsh Research Natural Area is nearby and researchers worry about the impact of machines on this ecosystem. Some of the horse trails in the vicinity were constructed to accommodate skiing. Additional ski trails are planned. The 15 mile round trip from the Sno-Park keeps the skiing opportunities in this area out of the capabilities of most skiers without an overnight.

The distances along Trail No. 8100 from the Sno-Park are provided to aid you in planning trips.

Trail No. 830	1.5 miles
Red Rock Pass	3.1 miles
Trail No.8123	5.2 miles
Kalama Horse Camp	7.3 miles

Cross-country skiers will find it enjoyable to ski Trail No. 8100 to Red Rock Pass. There they can climb onto the lava flow and ski northward toward the mountain on Trail No. 238. This provides some great views of the mountain.

Trail No. 8123 (Trail No. 8100 to Sheep Canyon Trailhead)

Ungroomed, 13 miles round trip

Snowmobilers will want to extend their trip by including Trail No. 8123 to Sheep Canyon Trailhead. This will add 13 miles of ungroomed trail to the 15 miles of groomed Trail No. 8100. You'll enjoy stopping to see the winter scene at Kalama Springs. Also, take the old road to the west at the Blue Lake Trailhead to gain access to a mudfow that will allow you to obtain some pleasant views of the mountain.

West Fork Snowmobile Trail No. 243, (Sno-Park to Sno-Park)

Groomed, 12 miles round trip

This route consists of 1.5 miles on Trail No. 8100, 1.0 mile on Trail No. 830 and 3.5 miles of Trail No. 243. Trail No. 243 is the first trail on the Gifford Pinchot National Forest to be constructed cross-country for snowmobiles. This was done to allow users at the Marble Mountain Sno-Park to continue to access the snow trails on the west side after Road 83 was plowed for vehicle access to the new Sno-Park.

Marble Mountain Sno-Park

Parking for about 60 vehicles with trailers
Groomed trails for snowmobiling and skiing
Warming hut with picnic tables
Compost toilets, emergency telephone

This is where most of the winter recreation is happening in the Mount St. Helens area. The skiers and snowmobilers have worked together with the Forest Service to plan the best possible facilities. The results are a very comfortable and functional warming hut and parking area.

There is some difficulty for first time users to decide which trail to take out of the parking area. This may be because snowmobilers use one of the principle ski trails, Trail No. 244, to gain access to Trail No. 243. This also creates dangerous situations in the parking area from snowmobiles and skiers coming back into the parking area at a right angle to the vehicle traffic. Be sure to stop before proceeding into the parking area.

There are volunteer hosts each weekend at the warming hut. They Shovel snow, keep the fire burning in the wood stove, greet visitors and perform minor site maintenance. Some hosts also serve hot beverages and cookies. They may not sell them, but can ask for a donation.

There is limited opportunity for snow play. Children climb onto the roof of the building with all sorts of sliding devices. Many parents walk and pull their children on sleds on groomed Trail No. 8100.

Families discuss plans for having fun in the snow in front of the warming hut.

The most popular trail opportunities accessible from this Sno-Park are:

Trail No. 8300, (Sno-Park to the Lahar)

> **Groomed, 10 miles round trip, easy**

This is the primary groomed route for reaching other trails and opportunities. This is also where most of the contact between different types of users occurs. Snowmobilers should use this trail only to gain access to other areas. This will reduce impacts on skiers, snowshoers and parents pulling sleds along the first 2 miles.

The best experiences for snowmobilers are on the Lahar. The wet cement-like slurry of rocks, mud and water rushed down the slopes on May 18, 1980, clearing vast areas of all vegetation between the Muddy River and Pine Creek. Snowmobilers like to follow the mudflow northeast to the Plains of Abraham. This provides some unforgettable views of the mountain, Ape Canyon and Smith Creek. The trail on the mudflow is not marked. Snowmobiles are not permitted beyond Windy Pass.

It is about 17 miles round trip from Trail No. 8300 to Windy Pass, or a 27 mile round trip from the Sno-Park. There is a lot of opportunity for short side trips to viewpoints so plan on about an additional 5 miles for your trip. The Plains of Abraham serve as a run-out zone for many avalanches from the steep slopes above. Snow travelers need to always be watching for the potential of an avalanche in this area.

For your convenience the distance to key junctions along Trail No. 8300 are provided.

Trail No. 244A	0.5 mile
Trail No. 216B	1.2 miles
Trail No. 236	1.8 miles
Trail No.380	2.7 miles
Trail No. 236B	3.5 miles

Trail No. 8312 (Sno-Park to Marble Mountain)

Groomed, more difficult skiing, easy snowmobiling
3.0 miles to Four Corners
Ungroomed 2.5 miles to the summit, most difficult skiing
Groomed 9 mile loop from the Sno-Park

This groomed but winding trail leads to the summit of a dormant volcano, Marble Mountain. At Four Corners, 3 miles from the Sno-Park, the grooming follows Trail 380 for 3 miles to Trail No. 8300 to provide a groomed loop to the Sno-Park of about 9 miles. The Trail No. 8312 proceeds ungroomed for another 2.5 miles uphill from Four Corners to the viewpoint on top. The ungroomed section will be most difficult to many skiers. You'll be rewarded with excellent views of Mount St. Helens, Mount Hood, Mount Adams and Mount Rainier.

Wapiti Ski Loops, Trails No. 245A, B, C, D, G

4.2 miles of loops 1.2 miles Trail No. 245A loop, easy Other 3 miles, more difficult

There are four loops of varying lengths that provide access to flat terrain with good views of the mountain. These trails in conjunction with groomed Trails No. 8300 and Trail No. 8312 provide good opportunities for beginners.

Sasquatch Ski Loops, Trails No. 236, 236A, B

Total of 6.7 miles, mixed difficulty levels Recommended for more advanced skiers

This trail system requires at least an intermediate level of skill. It begins about 1.8 miles east of the Sno-Park on Trail No. 8300. It's also accessible from the Sno-Park by the Pine Martin Trail No. 245E which runs parallel to Trail No. 8300. If you want to be away from the snowmobiles, use Trail No. 245E.

The Sasquatch system provides 3 loop opportunities. The lowest and easiest loop combines part of Trail No. 236 with Trail No. 236B and Trail No. 8300 for a 3.2 mile loop. When you combine this with the 3.6 miles round trip from the Sno-Park to the trailhead, it makes a nice 6.8 mile experience.

The middle loop that takes in more of Trail No. 236 and all of Trail No. 236A is a more difficult experience. It's the grade of the old roads that the Trail follows that makes it difficult. It takes you to some very excellent views of the mountain. This loop is 2.4 miles. When combined with the 1.8 miles of Trail No. 8300 and 0.4 mile of Trail No. 236 to get to the start of the loop, it makes an interesting 6.8 mile round trip from the Sno-Park.

The upper loop is the most difficult and the longest. It is signed as Trail No. 236. The views are the best available in this area. It's 3.8

miles round trip from Trail No. 8300, or about 7.5 miles round trip from the Sno-Park.

June Lake Ski Trail No. 216B

> **1.2 miles to June Lake, most difficult**
> **1.7 miles to the junction with Trail No. 244, most difficult**

This trail is worth the effort to see June Lake with it's winter coat. The lake and waterfall are the most beautiful when frozen and covered with snow. It's about 1.2 miles to the Lake from Trail No. 8300, and another short 0.5 mile across an open snow field on top of a lava flow to join Trail No. 244. It's only 1.8 miles down Trail No. 244 to the Sno-Park. This makes a nice loop of about 4.5 miles.

Swift Ski Trail No. 244

> **1.8 miles, most difficult**

This trail takes off directly north out of the Sno-Park. It is the winter climbing route. Some experienced skiers will continue on up the open slope of the mountain from where the trail markers end and telemark back down.

The marked trail is only 1.8 miles to its junction with the June Lake Trail No. 216B. The first portion of this trail is shared with snowmobilers accessing the West Fork Snowmobile Trail No. 243.

Wakapish Sno-Park

> **Parking for 20 vehicles with trailers**
> **Warming hut, compost toilets**

This Sno-Park is accessed from Randle by taking Road 25 south for about 20 miles. Turn right onto Road 99 and almost immediately you turn into the Sno-Park. There are no trails marked with the standard blue or orange diamonds. The snowmobile and ski use is on the unplowed roads. These

The most popular route is Road 99 for about 6 miles to Bear Meadow Viewpoint. This provides good views of the mountain and the steaming crater. It's also possible to go beyond here when snow conditions will permit travel on the road bed. The snow sometimes will get too deep and dense along narrow places in the road. Snowmobiles have a tendency to slide down across these steeply sloped snow banks and off the road.

Some users take Road 25 south to Elk Pass and ski or snowmobile east on The snowplay opportunities are good at the Sno-Park with users sliding on a Road 2551.hill near the parking area.

Scientists monitoring Mount St. Helens from Harrys Ridge. A new trail will allow visitors to hike to this location when SR 504 is completed to Johnston Ridge. (Geological Survey Photo)

Chapter 9   Looking into the Future

Avoiding Indifference

> **When we want to determine what will happen in the future we often find it beneficial to examine the past.**

In 1975, Spirit Lake and Mount St. Helens were one of the most popular destinations in the Pacific Northwest. The 124 unit campground on the shoreline was completely full all summer. Every weekend hundreds of potential visitors were disappointed to find all the camping spaces full. The Forest Service was in the process of planning a seven million dollar upgrade and expansion.

About the same time Geological Survey geologists, Dwight (Rocky) Crandell, Donal R. Mullineaux and Meyer Rubin, published a report that stated that Mount St. Helens was the one volcano in the conterminous United States most likely to reawaken and to erupt, "perhaps before the end of this century." Their forecast was based on the historic eruptive behavior of the mountain. They put this record together through radiocarbon dating of plant remains buried in or beneath the ash layers and other volcanic deposits.

The Forest Service didn't know how to react to the forecast. Perhaps it's difficult to imagine the power of a volcanic eruption until you actually see one. In early 1980 planning for the expansion was continuing.

The point of recounting the above is not to embarrass anyone, but to point out that humans tend to ignore the potential for harm from natural disasters. We tend to build our homes in the flood plains, along eroding coastlines, in tornado zones, and on the slopes of mountains. When nature does its thing we always seem surprised.

In the case of Mount St. Helens we must work hard to avoid this kind of indifference in the future. Future eruptions may not provide as long of a warning or be as small as the 1980 eruption. We need to learn from the 1980 eruption and avoid mistakes that could cost lives and increase destruction of property in the future.

Monitoring

In 1974 Congress passed legislation making the Geological Survey the lead Federal Agency responsible for providing reliable and timely warnings of volcanic hazards. Under this mandate, and recognizing the need to maintain systematic surveillance of Mount St. Helens after the eruption, the Geological Survey has established a permanent regional office at Vancouver, WA. This facility, the Cascade Volcano Observatory, is used by scientists to monitor Mount St. Helens for renewed activity and also to monitor other volcanoes of the Cascade Range in Washington, Oregon and northern California.

Scientists from the Cascade Volcano Observatory are continuously monitoring Mount St. Helens for signs of renewed eruptive activity. Some of these signs are:

> Increased earthquake activity recorded on seismographs monitored both by the University of Washington Geophysics Program and the Cascade Volcano Observatory.

> Swelling of the lava dome is routinely measured from nearby points with electronic measuring devices.

> Between 1980 and 1986 scientists monitored for changes in composition of gas collected from fumeroles and in gas emissions collected by aircraft. Presently the sulfur dioxide level is too low to detect and gas monitoring has been discontinued.

Experience since 1980 indicates that this monitoring is sufficient to detect the movement of new magma that must take place before an eruption will occur. Scientists of the Geological Survey believe that a significant eruption, one that would require the movement of a large volume of new magma, would be detected early enough to issue warnings and evacuate the potential hazard areas. Scientists can not predict explosions caused by ground water coming into contact with the hot lava dome and conduit rocks, or release of gas caused by crystallization of magma. This makes entry into the crater a risk.

Forecast by Geologists

"Mount St. Helens is virtually certain to erupt again, but its behavior in the past has been sufficiently varied that we have no well-established basis for forecasting the exact timing or nature of its next eruptive activity." This is the opening statement of a report on Volcanic Hazards prepared by the Geological Survey in 1992. It also states, "it is unclear whether the 1980 to 86 eruptions represent a complete but brief eruptive period or an early stage of a more prolonged eruptive period."

Let's take a look at the recent eruptive history of Mount St Helens.

- 1980 to 1986 - most recent eruptive activity

- dormant interval of approximately 120 years

- 1800 to 1857 - Goat Rocks eruptive period

- dormant interval of 30 years

- 1480 to about 1770 - Kalama eruptive period

- dormant interval of 600 to 700 years

According to the report, renewed eruptive activity could include one or a combination of the following:

♦ **Resumption of dome growth**

A plug has probably formed in the conduit beneath the dome. The pressure necessary to overcome this blockage may exceed that of any of the dome building eruptions since 1980. If dome growth resumes, it probably will be explosive initially to remove this blockage. This explosion will propel rocks probably northward because of the volcano's shape. A comparable blast occurred about 1200 years ago when the Sugar Bowl dome on the north flank of the mountain exploded. It propelled rock fragments up to 7 miles from the dome. It is assumed that a blast of the present lava dome could perform in like manner.

This would cause damage to facilities and injury to people up to perhaps seven miles to the north. The movement of magma necessary to produce the explosion would allow adequate warning to evacuate the hazard area. The buildings at Johnston Ridge and Coldwater Ridge could be damaged. The windows are high risk for breakage.

◆ Tephra Fall

In the event of an explosive eruption, volcanic ash and larger fragments, collectively called tephra, are ejected upward from the vent. The larger fragments fall close to the vent while smaller particles are driven long distances by the winds. The volume of these tephra falls will depend on the size of the event. It may be that only the flanks of the mountain get dusted with fine ash. On the other hand, a large magmatic eruption such as one that occurred at the end of the 15th century deposited ash about five feet deep at a distance of about six miles from the vent.

The wind direction during the eruption would determine where the ash falls. The prevailing winds at Mount St. Helens are from southeasterly to northeasterly. The hazard from ash fall is mostly to buildings which can collapse under the weight of the ash, particularly if the weight is increased by water from rain. The ash makes driving almost impossible. When the fine ash dries it is remobilized by every passing vehicle into a cloud that reduces visibility to near zero. It can block the air filter on your car and damage some of the running parts. It can also cause eye irritation or respiratory problems.

The buildings at Coldwater Ridge and Johnston Ridge were designed for withstanding an ash fall. Ash removal would be needed to keep roads passable.

♦ Lahars and Associated Flooding

A growing volume of snow and ice is accumulating between the lava dome and the crater walls. In 1992 it was estimated that about 40 million cubic meters were there. Renewed eruptive activity has the potential to rapidly melt all of this snow causing a significant lahar in the North Fork Toutle Valley and flooding downstream.

Portions of Loowit Trail No. 216 and Truman Trail No. 207 north of the crater would be destroyed. Other damage would be light as new facilities downstream were relocated out of the flood plain. The sediment retention dam would reduce the flooding potential farther downstream.

Lahars could also originate on the outer flanks of the mountain in the event that pyroclastic flows occurred when the slopes were covered with their deepest winter snow. Roads could be damaged at stream crossings.

♦ Lava Flows

Lava flows more fluid than those that built the lava dome have issued several times from Mount St. Helens. It would be more likely that a lava flow would issue from a vent within the crater than from a vent on the outer flank of the volcano. If this happens the lava flow would be directed out of the crater into the low areas between there and Spirit Lake.

The lava flow would damage the portions of Loowit Trail No. 216 and Truman Trail No. 207 in the low area north of the crater. Lava flows would generally not be life-threatening because they move so slowly that people can walk away from them.

♦ Pyroclastic Flows

These are hot, fast moving avalanches of gas-charged, dry pyroclastic debris such as ash, pumice and rock fragments discharged during an explosive event. They are produced by the fallback and downslope movement of fragments from an eruption column, or by the direct frothing-over at the vent. They are extremely destructive and deadly because of the high temperature and mobility. They usually move at velocities of about 100 mph.

The greatest danger is in the area north of the crater. In a very large eruption pyroclastic flows could pose a severe hazard over most of the area from Mt. Margaret Ridge south to Swift Reservoir.

Worst Case Scenario

Those of us doing the Comprehensive Management Plan for the Monument used to joke about the worst case scenario being that the volcano would return to a long period of dormancy. This would reduce interest in visiting the facilities at the end of SR 504 since the area is growing a new forest.

Imagine visiting the devastated area several decades from now. Everyone who witnessed the awesome power unleashed on May 18, 1980, will have gone away, except for those who were very young children. The Geological Survey has reduced the monitoring to almost zero after 50 years of no renewed activity. No one in the Forest Service experienced the 1980 eruptions. The political pressure is very strong to construct SR 504 through the Spirit Lake Basin and construct more conventional recreation facilities such as campgrounds and boating areas on the shoreline of Spirit Lake.

The highway is finally approved and constructed. During the next several decades, 2040 to 2060, a new visitor center is built on the shoreline of Spirit Lake since the views at existing visitor centers are becoming obscured by forests. Also the views are so much better of the lake and mountain. The aging facilities at Coldwater Lake and Johnston Ridge are closed and removed.

Spirit Lake is stocked with fish and boating is allowed. After a few years additional facilities are constructed on the shore including more traditional camping and picnicking. The area around the lake becomes the most visited place in the region for recreation.

About the year A.D. 2090 the mountain erupts without warning killing hundreds and destroying the facilities. The next cycle of humans responding to Mount St. Helens begins.

Preferred Scenario

Based on the data being collected by the Geological Survey and other scientists it appears possible that Mount St. Helens in 1980 began a long period of eruptive activity that will last for a century or more. The past history has almost always consisted of long periods of eruptive activity containing short periods of quiet.

The immediate threat is in the crater since the Geological Survey cannot predict the explosions caused when water from snow melt seeps into the hot material in the lava dome. These explosions hurl small boulders for up to 0.6 mile, and sometimes produce pyroclastic flows. The hazard is within the crater area and can be managed by permitting entry into the crater only to those monitoring the mountain and properly equipped.

Humans have demonstrated throughout history that they tend to ignore the potential for natural disasters, especially when it is a long time between events. This is evident from all the industry and houses built in the flood plains, seashores and on the slopes of volcanoes. The best scenario for Mount St. Helens could be about as follows: During the next decade the shifting of the Juan de Fuca Plate and the North American Plate provide the pressure necessary to remove the plug that has formed in the vent beneath the dome. Maybe this will be when the 9.0 or greater earthquake that's been predicted off the coast of Washington occurs. The lava dome blows away. Rocks the size of grapefruit land on Johnston Ridge and smaller pieces at Coldwater Lake.

The explosion propels tephra into the stratosphere for perhaps as high as 15 miles above the volcano. The prevailing winds drive the ash to the northeast depositing 2 to 3 feet of ash in Spirit Lake. The towns of Packwood and Randle receive a light dusting of ash.

The extreme heat in the crater instantly melts the snow that has accumulated and produces a mud flow that runs north generally, following Loowit Creek and eventually flowing into Spirit Lake.

The Geological Survey is able to issue warnings about two weeks in advance of eruptions. No one is injured during the eruption. Damage to the visitor facilities is very light. The roads and trails to the east require ash removal. Several windows are broken in the buildings at Coldwater Lake and Johnston Ridge. Portions of the Loowit Trail No. 216 and the Truman Trail No. 207 are destroyed.

The renewed eruptive activity receives world wide media coverage. The public is excluded from the area for about a month while repairs are made at Coldwater Lake and Johnston Ridge. The renewed interest by the world to see this volcano creates more demand than the facilities at Coldwater Lake and Johnston Ridge are able to handle. Time limits are placed on visitors to reduce the traffic jams near the end of SR 504. The increased tourism is a big boost to the local economy which is still hurting from the reduced timber harvest in the region. Funding for research which had completely disappeared during the quiet years is restored and the Geological Survey is adequately financed to increase monitoring here and throughout the Cascade Range.

The author wakes up from his favorite dream and decides it's time to move on to Chapter 10.

Mount St. Helens Trivia

The visible cone of the mountain was all formed during the past 2500 years. A forerunner of Spirit Lake was born about 3500 years ago when eruption debris formed a natural dam across the North Fork of the Toutle River.

Mount St. Helens is a stratovolcano. Stratovolcanoes are formed by layers upon layers of material ejected from the volcano or from lava flows which extrude from the crater or vent.

Chapter 10 Accommodations and Other Support Services

Lodging and Restaurants

Most visitors to the Mount St. Helens National Volcanic Monument come from out of the Pacific Northwest Region, and about 15 percent come from out of the United States. These visitors will need to eat and sleep while enjoying the scenery. This chapter is designed to help you find the best opportunities for high guality and value inns, campgrounds and restaurants. First, I'll provide you with suggestions on how to plan your trip to get the most out of your time and money.

If you're coming to the northwest for the first time, you should plan at least three days to visit the Monument. You'll also want to experience some of the other prime attractions of the area. If you're flying, your choice of either Seattle or Portland as your destination will determine which of these other attractions you'll want to include in your itinerary.

If you chose Portland, I suggest visiting one or more of these attractions:
- Columbia River Gorge with Multnomah Falls and Bonneville Dam
- Mount Hood with the historic Timberline Lodge
- Oregon Coast with its cliffs and sand dunes
- Ride on a sternwheeler on the Willamette or Columbia Rivers
- Local Portland attractions including Washington Park and Zoo, the World Forestry Center, and Oregon Museum of Science and Industry
- Fort Vancouver National Historic Site in Vancouver, WA

If you fly to Seattle, you may want to select one or more of these attractions:
- Mount Rainier National Park
- Olympic National Park

- Local Seattle attractions including Seattle Center with the Space Needle, Pike Street Market, Pioneer Square, and ferry rides on Puget Sound
- Cross the border by ferry or Interstate 5 to Victoria or Vancouver, Canada and experience the rich European flavor of these cities
- Cross the Cascade Mountains on State Route 2 to Leavenworth, WA and enjoy a Bavarian atmosphere

Some visitors fly into Portland, rent a car, and take in the local attractions, spend a few days around Mount St. Helens, a day at Mount Rainier, and drop off the rental car when they fly out of Seattle. The following suggested trip itinerary is based on this type of visit.

Sample Trip Itinerary for a Seven Day Visit

Day one

Fly into Portland International Airport
Spend the first night at either the Residence Inn by Marriott or Red Lion Inn at the Quay in Vancouver, WA
Participate in light sight seeing activities or shopping at the nearby malls. (Include Fort Vancouver National Historic Site.)
Eat your evening meal at the restaurant at the Quay and enjoy the well-done nautical theme.

Day two

Take a drive in the Columbia River Gorge. Plan to drive up the Washington side of the river on US 14 and visit the Pendelton Woolen Mill Outlet at Washougal, WA, the visitor center at Bonneville Dam, and cross the Columbia River at the Bridge of the Gods. Follow Interstate 84 west for about 5 miles where you'll find the Columbia River Gorge Scenic Highway. Turn onto it and enjoy 11 magnificent waterfalls including one of the highest in the United States, the 620 foot Multnomah Falls. Be sure to stop and visit the interpretive center and Inn. There's a good gift shop and an excellent restaurant in this historic building. Continue west on this interesting highway that was the first paved road in Oregon. It was designed like many of the European highways to blend into the steep landscape. At the Vista House you'll be rewarded with a panoramic view of the Columbia River. A little farther on at the

Women's Forum State Park you'll have a delightful view of the Vista House with the Columbia River in the background.

Continue west to return to Interstate 84 near Troutdale. You may wish to plan your trip so that you'll be ready for a dinner of chicken and dumplings at an excellent restaurant, Tad's, along the Sandy River between the Vista House and Troutdale. If you pass up Tad's, you'll have several excellent eating opportunities within walking distance of either Inn. (The Crossing, Who Song and Larry's, and the Chart House near the Quay, and the Olive Garden, Tony Romas, and the Red Lobster near the Residence Inn.)

Spend the night at either the Residence Inn or Red Lion Inn at the Quay. Make reservations for spending the next night at either the Red Lion Inn at Kelso, WA or the Mount St. Helens Inn at Castle Rock.

Day three

You'll spend the day on the south slopes of the mountain. Drive north on Interstate 5 for 20 miles to Woodland and turn onto SR 503. You'll want to visit Ape Cave Interpretive Site, the Trail of Two Forests Interpretive Site and Lava Canyon. Plan to eat dinner at either the Oak Tree in Woodland or at the Red Lion Inn at Kelso.

Day four

If you stay in Kelso, before leaving town, take about 30 minutes to enjoy the Mount St. Helens Visitor Center operated by the Kelso Chamber of Commerce. Then proceed north on Interstate 5 to exit 49 at Castle Rock and turn east onto SR 504. Drive east for about 5 miles to the Mount St. Helens Visitor Center.

Plan to spend at least two hours here. Be sure to see both of the audiovisual programs as they will help you to understand what you see at the Monument.

Drive about 40 miles east to the Coldwater Ridge Visitor Center. Plan to spend the rest of the afternoon in the area hiking. As you return west on SR 504 consider taking the helicopter flight over the blast area.

Plan to spend the night at the Mount St. Helens Motel or Timberland Motor Inn at Castle Rock.

Day five

Drive north on Interstate 5 to exit 68 and turn east on US 12. If you didn't pick up breakfast at the Rose Tree Restaurant, you'll find Spiffy's at this exit an excellent place for breakfast. Continue east on US 12 for approximately 50 miles to Randle. Turn left onto Road 25 and follow the signing to Windy Ridge Viewpoint. Plan to take in the interpretive talk.

As you back track on Road 99 stop at all the viewpoints and read the interpretive signs. Hike the Harmony Falls Trail No. 224 for 1.1 miles to Spirit Lake. You'll be rewarded with the view on the cover.

Hike the short trail to Meta Lake. Drive a short distance on Road 26 to Ryan Lake Viewpoint. Continue on Road 26 to the Quartz Creek Big Trees No.219 Interpretive Site and hike the trail through the big Douglas-fir trees. Return to Road 99 and stop at the Iron Creek Picnic Area to hike the short trail through old-growth trees.

Stay at the Cowlitz River Lodge in Packwood. Make reservations for dinner at the Chateau Inn 4 miles east of town.

Day six

Eat an early breakfast at Peter's Inn in Packwood. Drive east on US 12 and turn onto SR 123 and drive north into Mount Rainier National Park. Admission to the park is $5.00 per car which allows access into the park for 7 days. You can use your Golden Eagle Passport or Golden Age Passport.

Follow this road to the Sunrise Visitor Center for some great views of Mount Rainier. Return south on SR 123 and go west through Stevens Canyon to Paradise Inn. Enjoy your day hiking the trails at timberline and exploring the historic inn and the Henry Jackson Visitor Center. Make your reservations for Paradise Inn or the National Park Inn at Longmire well in advance as these old inns are very popular.

Day seven

Enjoy an early morning hike at timberline and keep your eyes open for wildlife. Drive west to Interstate 5 and go north to Seattle. Check in at the Doubletree Inn or Courtyard by Marriott at South Center via exit 153. Drive into the downtown area and visit the Pike Street Market and Space Needle. Eat fresh sea food at Ivar's Restaurant on the waterfront just below the market. Ask for a window seat and watch the ferry boats. Plan dinner for around sunset and you'll have another memorable experience.

Day eight

Your accommodations are close to Sea-Tac Airport and you'll find plenty of attractions to enjoy in the Seattle area until your flight leaves. Plan to spent a couple of days and learn history at the Klondike Gold Rush National Historical Park and the Underground Tour at Pioneer Square. Watch Mount St. Helens erupt on the Omnidome screen at the Aquarium, ride one of the harbor tours, or visit the Pacific Science Center.

The accommodations suggested above are in the moderate to high price segment of the market. If your interest is in more economy, study the following Directory for lodging and food and pick out something in your price range.

Lodgings and Restaurants Directory

Accommodations and dining are extremely important for making your trip to Mount St. Helens an enjoyable experience. In the following section you'll find the best lodging and dining opportunities available around the Mount St. Helens National Volcanic Monument.

There is a wide spectrum of opinions on what constitutes the best lodging. Some of us are satisfied with clean and comfortable rooms at a modest price while others are willing to pay a high price for luxury and sophistication. Most visitors to the monument are somewhere in the middle looking for a good balance of economy, quality, and comfort. This guide does not list all the possible accommodations available. Large franchises of economy motels such as Motel 6 or Super 8 are numerous along the Interstate 5 corridor and in the larger cities and are not mentioned. All the accommodations listed in this directory have been checked. If an accommodation in any of the small towns near the Monument was believed to be a poor value it does not appear in this directory.

Lodging and Restaurant Directory

Along Interstate 5

Packwood

Lodging

1st choice for lodging

Cowlitz River Lodge

Open all year, 32 units all air-conditioned with TV, telephone and hot tub. At $50.00 to $60.00 per night with continental breakfast it's a great value.

Make your reservations well in advance for the summer. Non-smoking rooms available.

(206) 494-4444 or Cowlitz River Lodge, 13069 US. Hwy. 12, Packwood, WA 98361.

Hotel Packwood

Built in 1912, this hotel is the oldest building in town. The hotel offered the finest accommodations and served as host to Teddy Roosevelt for his ascent of Mount Rainier. All rooms are newly renovated and are redecorated with antiques, new beds featuring comforters by local artists and cable TV. Two rooms have private baths while seven rooms share spacious baths. There are also rustic cabins. A single room with a shared bath is $18.00. The most expensive room is $35.00. Totally non-smoking. No pets. Hot tub. They do not take credit cards.

(206) 494-5431 or Hotel Packwood, Post Office Box 130, 102 Main St., Packwood, WA 98361.

Inn of Packwood

Formerly the Royal Inn. This motel has rooms with one queen bed for up to two people for $53.00 and two queen beds for up to four people for $65.00. They also have house keeping units for up to six people for $85.00. Indoor pool and hot tub.

(206) 494-5500 or Inn at Packwood, 1302 US Hwy. 12, P.O. Box 390, Packwood, WA 98361.

Mountain View Lodge Motel

This nice quiet motel has 22 rooms of various sizes and prices. They range from one person per room with a double bed at $28.00 to four people per room with two queen beds, kitchen, and fireplace at $76.00. There is an outdoor pool and hot tub.

(206) 494-5555 or Mountain View Lodge Motel, P.O. Box 525, Packwood, WA 98361.

Peter's Inn

There are three comfortable rooms above the Restaurant. They rent for $43.00 per night for a single and $53.00 per night for two people.

(206) 494-4000 or Peter's Inn, 13051 US. Hwy. 12, Packwood, WA 98361.

Restaurants

Ist choice for eating

Chateau Inn

This new restaurant located about 4 miles east of town on US 12 is the best place to eat in Packwood. They have prime rib, steaks, seafood, chicken and pasta. Prices range from $10.00 to $13.00. Bar. Opens at 4 p.m.

(206) 494-9224.

Peter's Inn

Located within walking distance of the Cowlitz River Lodge, Inn at Packwood and the Packwood Hotel, this is a favorite place to eat for the locals. Prices average about $10.00 for dinner. Senior discount. Bar and entertainment. Open Sun.-Thurs., 5 a.m.-9 p.m. and Fri. and Sat., 5 a.m.-10 p.m. When you make your reservations ask to be seated in the dinning room.

(206) 494-4000

Randle

Lodging

Cispus Conference and Learning Center

This facility which is operated by the Association of Washington School Principals and Educational Service District 113 is primarily a group facility. It also can accommodate individuals and families in a three bedroom house, a three bedroom trailer, and a two bedroom trailer. There are 21 sites for RV's. They can handle groups of up to 250 people. Group housing is in seven dormitories. All visitors must bring their own bedding. Call the Cispus Center for group rates. The RV sites are $11.00 per night with hookup and $7.00 per night with no hookup. The two bedroom trailer is $25.00 per night, the three bedroom trailer is $28.00 per night, and the three bedroom house is $46.00 per night.

(206) 497-7131 or Cispus Center, 2332 Cispus Road, Randle, WA 98377.

Morton

Lodging

1st choice

Seasons Motel

This is a nice 50 unit motel by the same company that owns the Cowlitz River Lodge in Packwood. At $50.00 to $60.00 per night with continental breakfast, it's a good value. Make reservations well in advance.

(206) 496-6835 or Seasons Motel, 200 Westlake Avenue, Morton, WA 98356.

St. Helens Manorhouse

Four rooms, two with private bath and two with shared bath. This is an old house built in 1910 and refurbished recently for a bed and breakfast. Family style country breakfast. Non-smoking. No children or pets. $36.00 to $42.00 for shared bath and $42.00 to $49.00 for private bath. Reservations are recommended in the summer months and are required between November 1 and April 31. Visa and MasterCard.

(206) 498-5243 or St. Helens Manorhouse, 7476 US Hwy. 12, Morton, WA 98356.

Restaurant

Roadhouse Inn and Hiway Room

About one mile west of Morton on US Hwy. 12 is a nice place for family dining. There is a large salad bar and fine steaks and seafood on the menu. Prices are average with dinner at about $10.00. Senior discount.

(206) 496-5029 or Roadhouse Inn, P.O. Box 490, Morton, WA 98356.

Salkum

Lodging

The Shepherd's Inn

Located 13 miles east of Interstate 5 on US 12 near Mayfield Lake and the Cowlitz River, this newly constructed 5,000 sq. ft.. country home has rooms with either queen or twin beds and private or shared baths. Two person jacuzzi. The breakfast features huckleberry crepes. Check in between 3:00 and 8:00 p.m. Rates are $50.00 to $55.00 per night for two or $45.00 to $50.00 per night for a single. Non-smoking. No children or pets. No credit cards.

(206) 985-2434 or The Shepherds Inn, 168 Autumn Heights Drive, Salkum, WA 98582.

Along State Route 703 to Mount Rainier National Park

Ashford

Lodging

Nisqually Lodge

This is a real nice 24 unit motel by the same owners as the Seasons Motel and Cowlitz Lodge, but a little higher priced because of the location near the National Park. It's AAA rated. Continental breakfast included. Rooms are priced from $65.00 to $80.00 during the summer.

(206) 569-8804 or Nisqually Lodge, Mt. Rainier, 31609 SR 706, Ashford, WA 98304.

Alexander's Country Inn

Renovated 1912 historic inn with many period furnishings. Thirteen units priced at $65.00 to $80.00 per night during the summer. Located about 1 mile from the Nisqually entrance to the Park. Whirlpool and hot tub. Weekend rates are less.

(206)569-2300.

!st choice for new visitors

Paradise Inn

Overlooking the valley at an altitude of 5,400 feet, this inn of 126 rooms built in 1917 offers an unequalled view of Mount Rainier and Nisqually Glacier. You'll enjoy the massive wooden beam construction, stone fireplaces and parquet wood floors. Open from late May through early October. Modern guest rooms are available with or without bath, and for smoking or non-smoking. Prices are $82.00 for up to two people for a room with private bath, and $58.00 for a room without the bath. Make reservations early as they fill up months ahead.

For information on reservations call (206) 569-2275 or write to Mount Rainier Hospitality Services, Star Route, Ashford, WA 98304.

National Park Inn

This small historic inn of 25 rooms with or without baths is open all year. It was built in 1926 and recently renovated to offer modern decor while retaining the historic ambience. There is a lounge, dining room, snack bar and gift shop. Non-smoking. Prices are about $76.00 per night for up to two people with bath and $54.00 per night for up to two people without private bath.

For reservations call (206) 569-2275 or write to Mount Rainier Hospitality Services, Star Route, Ashford, WA 98304.

Restaurants

1st choice

Alexander's Country Inn

Dining room in the historic inn with many period furnishings. Relaxed country atmosphere. Homemade breads and desserts. You'll need reservations as it's extremely popular. Open 11:30 a.m. to 9:30 p.m. Closed Mon.-Thurs., Nov. 1 to April 30.

(206) 569-2300.

Along Interstate 5

Centralia and Chehalis

Lodging

Candalite Mansion Bed & Breakfast

This 6,500 sq. ft. home was built in 1903 for a local lumber baron. There are six beautiful bedrooms with either king-size, regular or twin-size beds. Either private or shared bath. Their full breakfast includes a variety of gourmet dishes, home baked bread, eggs and fresh fruit. Non-smoking. No children or pets. No credit cards. Rates are $50.00 per night and up.
Call (206) 736-4749 or Candalite Mansion, 402 N. Rock, Centralia, WA 98531.

Ferryman's Inn

This 84 unit inn is located at exit 82. Factory outlets are located near-by. Rooms are clean and well kept. There is a heated pool and indoor spa. Continental breakfast. Some kitchen units and units specially equipped for physically challenged guests. Conference facilities. Rates range from $54.00 per night for a room with one bed for two people to $63.00 per night for two beds and three people. Under 12 free. Senior discounts and AAA.
(206) 330-2094 or Ferryman's Inn, 1003 Eckerson Road, Centralia, WA 98531.

Huntley Inn

There are 87 comfortable, clean rooms and 32 have refrigerators. Located 2 blocks east of exit 82. Continental breakfast. Jacuzzi suites and outdoor heated pool. Non-smoking rooms. Rates are approximately $40.00 per night and up. AAA.
1-800-448-5544 or Huntley Inn, 702 West Harrison, Centralia, WA 98531.

1st choice in this area

Best Western Pony Soldier Motor Inn

Located off Interstate 5 at exit 76 this motor inn has 69 units all with queen beds and 64 with refrigerators. Heated outdoor pool and hot tub. Non-smoking rooms available. No pets. Continental breakfast. Meeting rooms. Rates range from $40.00 per night for a single to $48.00 per night for two people and two beds. AAA and senior discounts.

1-800-634-PONY or Pony Soldier Motor Inn, 122 Interstate Ave., Chehalis, WA 98532.

Restaurants

1st choice

Mary McCrank's

Established in 1935 this restaurant was rated by USA TODAY as one of the 10 best dinner houses in the nation. For many years it was in the top rated restaurants for Mobile Travel Guide and AAA. If you are returning from Mount St. Helens on US 12 turn north at Mary's Corner, about 3 miles from Interstate 5, onto the Jackson Highway. Drive north for about 6 miles to the restaurant. If you're in a motel ask for directions. Moderately priced. Home made bread and desserts. Closed Mondays. Open Sundays from noon to 8:00 p.m. and open Tues. to Sat. for lunch 11:30 a.m. to 2:30 p.m. and for dinner 5:00 p.m. to 8:30 p.m. Reservations advised.

(206) 748-3662, or Mary McCrank's, 2932 Jackson Highway, Chehalis, WA 98532.

Spiffy's

Located at exit 68 on Interstate 5, this has been a popular place to eat for a long time. They started out as a drive-up place to purchase hugh hamburgers, and has grown into a full service restaurant. It's a good place to eat breakfast when you start out for Mount St. Helens. It's also good for lunch or dinner. They are famous for Minnesota Rice soup. You can buy a bag of the rice to take home. Prices are moderate.

Castle Rock

Lodging

Mt. St. Helens Motel

Less than 0.25 mile east of Interstate 5 at exit 49, this is a reasonably priced, clean and comfortable place to stay. Ask for a room on the backside as there's early morning traffic on SR 504.

There are 32 units, all with queen-size beds. Restaurants and shops are nearby. Laundry facilities. Free morning coffee. Mount St. Helens Visitor Center is 5 miles east. Rates are $30.00 per night for a single, $38.00 per night for two people in one bed, and $48.00 per night for two people with two beds. Each additional person is $5.00.

(206) 274-7721, or Mt. St. Helens Motel, 227 Spirit Lake Hwy., Castle Rock, WA 98611.

Timberland Motor Inn

Located about one-eighth mile east of Interstate 5 at exit 49, this 17 unit motor inn is priced right for the services offered. Non-smoking rooms available. There are queen-size beds, small refrigerators, and free coffee and tea. There's a laundromat, beauty shop and "Unique Products of Washington" shop on site. AAA approved. Prices are $37.00 per night for a single, $43.00 per night for two people, and $62.00 per night for 4 people. Pets are extra.

(206) 274-6002 or Timberland Motor Inn, 206 Spirit Lake Hwy., Castle Rock, WA 98611.

Restaurants

Rose Tree Restaurant

This restaurant is within walking distance of the two motor inns listed above. They have a salad bar and a traditional menu of steaks, chicken and seafood. They also have a large dining room in back and can handle banquets. Prices are low to moderate.

Kelso & Longview

Lodging

Red Lion Inn

Located at exit 39 on Interstate 5, this is the best place to stay if you don't mind the extra cost. The 163 rooms are comfortable and the service is great. There's a heated pool and a whirlpool. There's a lounge with recorded music. They can accommodate groups and conventions of up to 600. Prices are $79.00 per night for a single, and $89.00 to $95.00 per night for two people. Ask for the special

weekend rate which is $69.00. AAA members get 10 percent discount, and AARP discount of 20 percent.
1-800-547-8010 or Red Lion Inn, 510 Kelso Drive, Kelso, WA 98626.

Comfort Inn

Located on the west side of Interstate 5 at exit 39 behind the Three Rivers Mall, this new inn has 57 comfortable, spacious and clean rooms at moderate prices. Special rooms are available for the physically challenged. Choice of single queen, double queen mini-suites and deluxe queen and king suites complete with sofa sleeper, microwave, refrigerator and whirlpool tubs. Non-smoking rooms are available. There is an indoor pool and spa. Continental breakfast included. Prices are $45.00 to $60.00 per night for a single or $50.00 to $65.00 per night for two people.
(206) 425-4600 or Comfort Inn, 440 Three Rivers Drive, Kelso, WA 38626.

Restaurants

1st choice for value and view

Charlie's

This low to medium priced restaurant is in a beautiful location, and visitors staying in the Kelso-Longview area should take advantage of it. It's easy to access from the motels mentioned above. Just take the main street into Kelso and follow it across the river into Longview. Turn left at the Longview end of the bridge onto First Avenue. It's only a couple of blocks to Charlie's. You'll be pleased with the location right on the Cowlitz River. They're open Sunday through Thursday from 6:00 a.m. to 9:00 p.m. and Friday and Saturday from 6:00 a.m. to 10:00 p.m. The menu includes steaks, seafood, chicken, and pasta. You'll be shocked by the low price of the Northwest and California wines offered. They are also a full service bakery. When you make your reservation ask for a table over-looking the river.
(206) 636-5661 or Charlie's, 1826 First Avenue, Longview, WA 98632.

Woodland

Lodging

Woodlander Inn

This 61 unit inn just off of Interstate 5 at exit 21 is in a good location for lodging when you visit the south side of Mount St. Helens. The rooms are clean and have queen size beds. Non-smoking rooms are available. An indoor pool and spa were added in 1992. Rates are $42.00 per night for a single, $46.00 per night for two people for one bed, and $50.00 per night for two people for two beds. Winter season rates are less. AAA and senior discounts.
1-800-444-9667 or Woodlander Inn, 1500 Atlantic Street, Woodland, WA 98674.

Restaurants

Top choice

Oak Tree Restaurant

Prior to the 1980 eruption of Mount St. Helens, my office was at the ranger station at Amboy and I supervised the operation of the campgrounds at Spirit Lake. It was a two hour drive each way to the lake and I often stopped at the Oak Tree Restaurant for breakfast or dinner. It's an excellent place to eat and a good value. It's located at exit 21 on the east side of the freeway. They serve the usual array of steaks, seafood, chicken and pasta. They're famous for Bankrupcy Stew and Oak Tree Salad. Sunday Brunch. Moderately priced.
(206) 887-8661.

Yale and Cougar

Lodging

Lone Fir Resort

This is as close as you can get to the south side of the mountain and stay in comfortable lodging. There are a total of 16 rooms available. Three are cabins, two units are in a house, and some are complete with kitchens. There is an outdoor pool. Rates are $38.00 per night and up. Open all year.
(206) 238-5210 or Lone Fir Resort, Cougar, WA 98616.

Anderson's Lodge

This is a family-run retreat center tucked in the hills about 23 miles east of Woodland. It's ideal for small groups such as reunions, churches and schools. The lodge rents by the weekend. Rates are reasonable at $12.00 for one night mid-week or $24.00 for two nights on the weekend during the summer. You'll need a group of at least 40 to rent the facility. Rates can be negoiated for larger groups. You can prepare your own food, eat at nearby restaurants, or use a catering service available through Anderson's. There is a Japanese soaking tub, hot tub, tennis courts, softball field, volleyball court, soccer field, horseshoe pits and outdoor amphitheater. It's a nice facility if you are coming to Mount St. Helens with a small group. Call for reservations.

(206) 693-1838 or Anderson's Lodge, 809 N. W. 59th St., Vancouver, WA 98663.

Vancouver

Lodging

1st choice for the rich and famous lifestyle
Residence Inn by Marriott

If you're into service, comfort and sophistication, and can afford it, you'll love the Residence Inn. The Vancouver Residence Inn is conveniently located across the river from the Portland Airport, along the route you'll need to follow to Mount St. Helens. Take Interstate 205 to the Battleground SR500 exit 30. Go west toward Vancouver on SR500 and proceed for about one mile. Turn right at the first light, Thurston Road, and left at the next light, only about 200 feet. The inn is on the left about 600 feet to the west. Airport transportation provided. There are 120 units priced as follows: Studio suite with a queen bed, living and kitchen area for $100.00 per night; Executive suite with a separate bedroom and a living and kitchen area for $115.00 per night; Penthouse CICO with a king size loft, a murry bed on the main floor and two baths for $135.00 per night; and the Penthouse double with a king size bed in the loft, a separate bedroom on the main floor and two baths for $145.00 per night.

(206) 253-4800.

Red Lion Inn at the Quay

This is my favorite place to direct visitors. It's a 160 room inn on the Columbia River next to the Interstate 5 bridges. Spectacular views. The service is always excellent and the decor fits the surrounding environment. The restaurant is excellent and there are several other excellent restaurants within walking distance. Heated outdoor pool, court yard and dock. Airport transportation. Rates are $87.00 to $101.00 per night for a single, and $102.00 to $123.00 per night for a double.
(206) 694-8341.

Ferryman's Inn

This inn of 133 comfortable and clean rooms is at a good location along Interstate 5 at the 78th Street exit in Hazel Dell. Some units have refrigerators. There's a heated pool and a coin laundromat. Good restaurants within walking distance. Rates are a good value; $54.00 per night for a queen bed and two people, $58.00 per night for two queen beds for two people, and $63.00 per night for three people. Children under 12 free. Pets are $3.00 extra.
(206) 574-2151.

Restaurants

1st choice in the Vancouver Area

Inn at the Quay

You'll enjoy the nautical theme of this restaurant from the railings and belaying pins at ground level to the ratlines, masts and starlit night sky above. It's worth coming into the restaurant or lounge to see these unique decorations even if you don't eat or drink here. The food and service are excellent. Their Sunday Brunch is one of the best in town and a good value. Plan to spend $10.00 to $18.00 per person for dinner and a lot less for lunch or brunch. Open 6 a.m. to 10 p.m., Sunday to Thursday, and until 11 p.m. Friday and Saturday.
(206) 694-8341 for reservations.

The Crossing

This unique restaurant allows you to relive the days when railroad travel was popular. Dine aboard classic railroad cars that represent a century of history. The food is good and the prices moderate.

There's a salad bar. Located in the downtown area at 900 West 7th Street.

(206) 695-3374 for reservations.

Hidden House

This is where we go when we want a quiet atmosphere and good food. The Hidden House was build in 1885 for the Hidden Family who made their fortune making the bricks that were important in the building construction at that time. Located downtown at 100 West 13th Street. Prices are moderate to high. They serve dinner Tues. through Sun. from 5 p.m. and lunch Mon. through Fri.

(206) 696-2847

Edelweiss

This German-American restaurant will leave you humming some of the old German folk songs that strolling musicans and singing waiters perform for you. The schnitzels are outstanding, including jager rahm, wiener, and cordon blue and are moderately priced. Located at 8800 N.E. Highway 99 in Hazel Dell. Take exit 4 off Interstate 5.

(206) 574-4984 for reservations.

Seattle

Lodging

Doubletree Inn

This inn has 200 comfortable and clean rooms located convenient to the Sea-Tac Airport. It's located at the Southcenter Shopping Mall and provides transportation to the airport. The service is good and there's a good restaurant on site and many other places to eat nearby. Prices are $71.00 to $94.00 per night for a single, $81.00 to $94.00 per night for two people for one or two beds. If you want more sophistication and elegance, the Doubletree Suites is located nearby and answers to the same phone number. AAA rated. Pets are $20.00,extra.

(206) 575-8220 or Doubletree Inn, 205 Strander Blvd., Seattle, WA 98188.

Hampton Inn - Southcenter

This newly constructed inn has 154 clean and comfortable rooms. Heated pool, whirlpool and exercize room. Airport transportation. Smoking and non-smoking rooms and free continental breakfast. Located at Southcenter. Prices are a good value at $50.00 to $61.00 per night for a single, and $60.00 to $71.00 per night for two people. Suites available.

(206) 228-5800 or 1-800-HAMPTON.

Residence Inn by Marriott

These accommodations are exactly like those in Vancouver and priced the same.

1-800-331-3131 or Residence Inn by Marriott-South, 16201 W Valley Hwy., Seattle, WA 98188.

Camping

Campground requirements vary greatly for each of us depending on our backgrounds and equipment. Some of us are happy to be in a very primitive setting with very limited facilities such as pit or vault toilets and no drinking water. Others prefer to travel in comfort and own or rent recreation vehicles (RV's), that contain most of the luxuries that we enjoy at home, flush toilet, shower, bed, electricity, heat, TV, etc. The following directory will help you to select a campground in-route to the attractions around the mountain that will best meet your needs.

The Mount St. Helens National Monument is located in the Gifford Pinchot National Forest. The National Forest System is the largest provider of dispersed recreation opportunities in the nation. Dispersed recreation is any recreation that occurs outside of developed sites such as campgrounds. You may camp any where in the National Forest that isn't designated as closed to camping on the forest map or signed closed on the ground. This type of camping may appeal to those who like the primitive experience or have a self-contained RV.

It's important that you understand that when you elect to camp outside a developed campground that you assume all the responsibility for anything that happens to you. The land owner is not liable for making this area safe; such as, by falling unsafe trees or signing hazards; so the risk is greater.

Also, you must carry a shovel, water bucket and ax if you build a fire. It's best not to build a fire if you elect this type of camping. Ask at the ranger station for their recommendation for a location for this type of camping. The blast area from the 1980 eruption is closed to camping.

Campground Directory

Along Interstate 5

Site #1   PARADISE POINT STATE PARK

Location: 15 miles north of Vancouver, WA on I-5.
Recommendation: This is a good backup site if campgrounds closer to the mountain are full or your arrival time does not permit driving closer.
Campsites, facilities:
- 70 sites for tents or self-contained RV's up to 45 feet long
- Piped water, flush toilets and showers
- Picnic tables and firewood
- Trailer Dump

Reservations, fee:
- Open all year, but weekends only during the winter, $8/night, no reservation necessary
- (206) 263-2350 or Paradise Point State Park, Route 1, Box 33914, Ridgefield, WA 98642

Site #2   LOUIS RASMUSSEN RV PARK

Location: Take Exit 30 off I-5 near Kalama, WA and drive 100 yards west crossing the railroad tracks then make a cloverleay south for 1.5 miles. It.s located on the bank of the Columbia River.
Recommendation: A good camp if you're unable to get closer to the mountain. Also, good if you're planning to recreate on the Columbia River.
Campsites, facilities:
- 50 tent sites, and 22 drive-through sites for RV's of any length
- Piped water, showers, flush toilets, sewer hookups and electricity
- Bottled gas, a store, food service, laundromat and ice within one mile
- Boat docks and launching nearby

- Pyramid Ales Brewery and small City Park adjacent to the North
- Pets and motorbikes ok

Reservations, fees;
- Open all year, $12/night for full hook-up, up to 4 people, $1 for each additional, $7/night for no hook-up or tents. Reservations.
- (206)673-2626, or Louis Rasmussen RV Park, P.O. Box 7, Kalama, WA 98625

Site #3   CAMP KALAMA RV PARK

Location: Take Exit 32 off I-5 near Kalama, WA and drive one block south on the Frontage Road and you'll see the campground.

Recommendation: This will serve nicely if you are unsure of a camping spot closer to the mountain. A good location if your plans include some recreation on the Columbia River.

Campsites, facilities:
- 30 tent sites and 87 sites for RV's of any length, 15 sites are pull-through type
- Piped water, showers, sewer hookups and electricity
- Bottled gas, ice, store, food service, laundromat and playground
- Full service marina nearby
- Pets and motorbikes ok

Reservations, fees:
- Open all year, reservations, $11.00/night for tents and $18.24/night including tax for sites with full hook-up
- MasterCard and Visa, AAA rated and senior discounts
- (206)673-2456 or Camp Kalama RV Park, 5055 North Meeker Drive, Kalama, WA 98625

Site #4   THE CEDARS RV PARK

Location: Take Exit 46, Headquarters Road, off I-5 and drive east to the first service road and proceed north to the park. Situated in a nice grove of tall cedars.

Recommendation: Use the campgrounds closer to the visitor center on SR 504. Use this if those are full.

Campsites, facilities:
- Three tent sites and 21 sites for RV's of any length
- Piped water, flush toilets, showers and electricity

- Bottled gas and laundromat
- Pets ok

Reservations, fees:
- Open all year, reservations, $13.00/night per site with full hook-up for two people, plus $1.00/each extra person over 10 years old, $8.00/night for tent site. (plus tax)
- (206)274-7019 or Cedars RV Park, 115 Beauvais Road, Kelso, WA 98626

Site #5   MERMAC STORE & RV PARK

Location: Take Exit 52 off I-5 and drive 100 feet to the park.
Recommendation: Use if other campgrounds closer to the visitor center are full.
Campsites, facilities:
- 10 sites for RV's of any length and 3 acres for tent camping
- Piped water, sewer hookups, flush toilets and showers
- Store and ice
- Pets ok

Reservations, fees:
- Open all year 8 a.m. to 8 p.m., reservations, $12.00/night for full hook-up or $6.50/night for tents including tax
- Call (206)274-6785 or Mermac Store & RV Park, 112 Burma Road, Castle Rock, WA 98611

Site #6   ESTES RV PARK

Location: Take Exit 57 off I-5 and drive west on Foster Creek Drive for 0.5 mile to the park. Located next to I-5 freeway.
Recommendation: Use if the other campgrounds closer to the visitor center are full. Excellent location for steelhead fishing.
Campsites , facilities:
- 20 tent sites and 20 drive-through sites for RV's of any length
- Piped water, sewer hookups, flush toilets, showers and electricity
- Food service, a store, bottled gas, ice and laundromat
- Boat docks nearby
- Pets and motorbikes ok

Reservations, fees:
- Open all year, reservations, $11/night

- American Express, MasterCard and Visa
- (206)864-2386 or Estes RV Park, 193 Foster Creek Drive, Toledo, WA 98591

Site #7   COWLITZ BEND

Location: Take Exit 59 off I-5 and drive west on highway 506 for 400 yards. Located next to I-5 freeway.

Recommendation: Use other sites closer to the visitor center if available. Check this out in the spring when the smelt are in the river. You'll enjoy watching the locals dipping their nets and filling them with these bony little fish.

Campsites, facilities:
- 20 tent sites and 24 drive-through sites for RV's of any length
- Piped water, flush toilets, showers and electricity
- Food service, laundromat, bottled gas, ice and a store are within one mile
- Boat launch nearby
- Pets and motorbikes ok

Reservations, fees:
- Open all year, reservations, $9/night
- (206)864-2895 or Cowlitz Bend, 491 Highway 506, Castle Rock, WA 98611

Site #8   FROST ROAD TRAILER PARK

Location: Take Exit 63 off I-5 near Winlock and drive 0.7 mile east to Henriot Road, turn left and go 1.6 miles to Frost Road, turn left on Frost Road 0.3 mile to the park. If you're coming south on I-5 take exit 68 and go east on US 12 for about 0.25 mile, take Meier Road south for 2.5 miles to Hart Road, turn right and drive about 0.25 mile to the camp. Nice wooded Douglas-fir setting.

Recommendation: My first choice would be the Lewis & Clark State Park but in the event that it's full and you want to be in this area this is a suitable alternative.

Campsites, facilities:
- 15 tent sites and 20 sites for RV's of any length
- Piped water, flush toilets, showers, sewer hookups and electricity
- Bottled gas, ice, laundromat and recreation hall

- Pets ok, except for big dogs

Reservations, fees:
- Open all year, reservations, $12.00/night for full hook-up and $8.00/night for tents. (plus tax)
- (206)785-3616 or Frost Road Trailer Park, 762 Frost Road, Winlock, WA 98596

Site #9   LEWIS AND CLARK STATE PARK

Location: Take Exit 68 off I-5 and drive 3 miles east on US 12, turn right and drive south on Highway 99 to the park. Beautiful forested setting.

Recommendation: This site could provide you with comfort on your way to Randle to see the Road 99/Windy Ridge attractions. This is an old-growth forest Park. There is a kids fishing pond stocked with trout and a 1.5 miles nature trail.

Campsites, facilities:
- 33 tent sites
- Piped water and flush toilets
- Playground
- Pets ok

Reservations, fees:
- Open all year, No reservations, $8.00/night
- (206) 864-2643 or Lewis and Clark State Park, 4583 Jackson Highway 99, Winlock, WA 98596

SOUTH OF MOUNT ST. HELENS/SR 503 ACCESS

Site #10   LEWIS RIVER RV PARK

Location: 4 miles east of Woodland, WA on State Route 503.

Recommendation: If you're interested in steelhead or salmon fishing, golfing, or Native American interpretation in addition to visiting the mountain this could be for you. One of the best 18 hole golf courses in SW Washington and Chief Lelooska's Coastal Indian long house is nearby.

Campsites, facilities:
- Over 80 sites for tents, trailers, RV's of any length
- Piped water, flush toilets, sewer hookups, showers and electricity

- Picnic tables, firewood, bottled gas and ice
- Cafe, store, laundromat and swimming pool
- Boat docks, launching and rentals nearby
- Pets ok

Reservations, fee:
- Open all year, reservations, $13.38/night, MasterCard and Visa
- (206) 225-9556 or Lewis River RV Park, 3125 Lewis River, Woodland, WA 98674

Site #11   VOLCANO VIEW CAMPGROUND

Location: 25 miles east of Woodland, WA on State Route 503, turn right at Jack's Restaurant for 1.5 miles.

Recommendation: This is a good backup site if campgrounds closer to the mountain are full. May be the right place if you're going to visit the southwest side of the mountain.

Campsites, facilities:
- 30 tent sites and 47 sites for RV's of any length
- Piped water, flush toilets, sewer hookups, showers and electricity
- Picnic tables, firewood and recreation hall
- Pets ok

Reservations, fee:
- Open all year, reservations, $14.00/night, plus tax, for full hook-up
- (206) 231-4329, or Volcano View Campground 230 Highway 503, Aerial, WA 98603

Site #12   LONE FIR RESORT

Location: 29 miles east of Woodland, WA on State Route 503 in Cougar, WA.

Recommendation: If you're in an RV and can make your reservation early, this is your best bet for visiting the attractions on the south side of the mountain. Also, the best accommodations for winter use on the south side.

Campsites, facilities:
- 5 tent sites and 27 sites for trailers and RV's of any length
- Piped water, flush toilets, sewer hookups, showers and electricity
- Swimming pool
- Boat docks and launching facilities nearby
- Pets ok

- Stores and cafe nearby

Reservations, fee:
- Open all year, reservations, $14.00/night for two people plus $2.00/ea. extra person/night, MasterCard and Visa
- (206) 238-5210 or Lone Fir Resort, Cougar, WA 98616

Site #13   MERRILL LAKE

Location: 28 miles east of Woodland, WA on State Route 503 to Forest Service Road 81, about 1 mile west of Cougar, WA. North on Road 81 for 4.5 miles.

Recommendation: On Merrill Lake, this is a great campground for those seeking a primitive setting or wanting to try their luck at fly fishing for trout. A good location for exploring the attractions on the southwest slopes of the mountain.

Campsites, facilities:
- 11 campsites for tents or small trailers
- Pit toilets, piped water, and firewood
- Picnic tables, fire grills and tent pads
- Boat launching

Reservations, fees:
- Open when snow free, no reservations, no fee
- 1-800-527-3305 or Dept. of Natural Resources, AW-11, 1065 South Capital Way, Olympia, WA 98504

Site #14   KALAMA HORSE CAMP

Location: Drive 28 miles east of Woodland, WA on State Route 503 to Forest Service Road 81, about 1 mile west of Cougar, WA. Proceed north on Road 81 for 9.4 miles.

Recommendations: If you have horses or don't mind sharing your campground with horses this may be the right place for you. The best horse riding in the Monument begins on the Toutle River Trail that starts here. The parking area also can be used in the Winter for a Sno-Park for both snowmobilers and cross-country skiers. Mosquitoes and flies are usually numerous until late June. Constructed by volunteers from the Backcountry Horsemen of WA, the WA Trail Riders Association and the Clark County Executive Horse Council. Please say thank you to the horse riders that you meet at this camp.

Campsites, facilities:
- 10 campsites for self-contained RV's (2 group sites, 2 single family sites and 6 double family sites)
- Compost toilets, stock water, but no potable water
- Special loading ramp for the physically challenged
- Corrals at each unit
- Trailhead parking for 20 vehicles with trailers

Reservations, fees:
- Open about May 1 through October, no fee, no reservations
- (206) 247-5473 or Monument Manager, Mount St. Helens National Volcanic Monument, 42218 NE Yale Bridge Road, Amboy, WA 98601

Site #15   CLIMBERS BIVOUAC

Location: Drive 28 miles east of Woodland, WA on State Route 503 to Forest Service Road 81, about 1 mile west of Cougar, WA. Proceed north on Road 81 for 12.6 miles to the junction of Road 8123 and Road 81, the last 0.5 mile should have been on gravel surface. Turn right on Road 81 for another 3.5 miles to the junction with Road 8100830. Turn left and continue uphill for 2.6 miles to the turn-around at the end of the road.

Recommendations: This is the most popular base camp for climbing Mount St. Helens. It's also excellent for taking off on the Loowit Trail No. 216, an around-the-mountain trail at timberline.

Campsites, facilities:
- Primitive camping, no defined campsites
- Compost type toilets, no water
- Emergency telephone

Reservation, fees:
- Open when the road is snow free, June 1 to October 31, no fee, no reservations but you need a permit to climb above timberline when the mountain is snow free
- (206) 247-5473 or Monument Manager, Mount St. Helens National Volcanic Monument, 42218 NE Yale Bridge, Amboy, WA 98601

Site #16   COUGAR CAMPGROUND

Location: From Woodland, WA drive 29.5 miles east on State Route 503 through Cougar to the campground entrance.

Recommendation: This is convenient to stores, cafes and other services in Cougar. It's also on Yale Reservoir and adjacent to a developed swimming and boating area. It's a top choice if you can get in. Come in late August and watch the Kokanee Salmon spawn in Cougar Creek. You'll find the Pacific Power and Light Co. campgrounds on the Lewis River Reservoirs to be well managed, a good value and an excellent place to camp.

Campsites, facilities:
- 45 tent sites and 15 sites for group camping
- Piped water, flush toilets and showers
- Picnic tables, firewood, grills
- Food service, ice, bottled gas nearby
- Swimming beach and boat launch adjacent
- Pets ok on leash

Reservations, fees:
- Open Memorial Day to Labor Day, no reservations, $8/night
- Call (503) 464-5024 or Pacific Power and Light Co., Recreation, 920 SW 6th Ave., Portland, OR 97204

Site #17   BEAVER BAY

Location: Drive 31 miles east on State Route 503 from Woodland, WA through Cougar to the Beaver Bay Campground on Yale Reservoir.

Recommendation: If you're interested in fishing or boating in addition to visiting the south side of the mountain this could be the spot for you. Kokanee Salmon fishing is good during the late summer and Yale Reservoir is a great place for sailing.

Campsites, facilities:
- 63 sites for tents and RV's
- 15 sites for group camping
- Piped water, flush toilets and showers
- Boat launching and docks
- Pets ok on leash
- RV sewage dump

Reservations, fees:
- Open April through November, no reservations, $8/night Memorial Day to Labor Day
- (503) 464-5024 or Pacific Power and Light Co., Recreation, 920 SW 6th Ave., Portland, OR 97204

Site #18   SWIFT FOREST CAMP

Location: Drive 48 miles east of Woodland, WA on State Route 503 and Forest Service Road 90 through Cougar, WA to the upper end of Swift Reservoir.

Recommendations: This is a good camp for those taking the Road 25/99 route to Windy Ridge and Spirit Lake. Excellent fishing for Rainbow and Dolly Vardin Trout.

Campsite, facilities:
- 93 campsites for tents and RV's
- Flush toilets, piped water and boat launch
- Emergency telephone at the nearby information station
- RV sewage dump
- Pets ok on leash

Reservations, fees:
- Open April through November, $8/night, no reservations
- (503) 464-5024 or Pacific Power and Light Co., Recreation, 920 SW 6th Ave., Portland, OR. 97204

Site #19   LOWER FALLS

Location: Drive 48 miles east of Woodland, WA on State Route 503 and Forest Service Road 90 through Cougar, WA to the upper end of Swift Reservoir to the junction of Roads 25/90. Continue to the right on Road 90 for 18 miles to the campground.

Recommendations: This is one of my favorite places and I'm sure it will become one of yours once you've camped here. Native Americans camped here to harvest salmon that bunched up at the Lower Falls, the first obstacle to their upstream migration before the three dams were built down stream. The 100 foot wide and 40 foot high waterfall is one of three within a mile stretch of the river upstream. A thrilling trail along the Lewis River provides easy access to all three falls.

Campsites, facilities:
- 43 campsites for tents or RV's
- Water by a hand pump
- Compost toilets
- Barrier-free trail to a viewpoint of the falls

Reservations, fees:
- Open April through October, no fee, no reservations, donations accepted
- (206) 247-5473 or Monument Manager, Mount St. Helens National Volcanic Monument, 42218 NE Yale Bridge Road, Amboy, WA 98601

Site #20   BATTLE GROUND LAKE

Location: About 8 miles north of Vancouver, WA on I-5 take the Fairground Exit 7 and drive 2 miles north to Duluth. Turn right (east) on State Route 502, continue for 8 miles straight through Battle Ground to Al and Ernie's Market at Grace Street and turn left (north) for 1.5 miles to the campground.

Recommendations: This state park has horseback riding trails and some primitive campsites that will accommodate campers with horses. It's a good lake for swimming and fishing. A good location for a base to explore the south side of the mountain, and only about 15 minutes off I-5.

Campsites, facilities:
- 35 sites for tents or self-contained RV's up to 50 feet long
- Piped water, Flush toilets and showers
- Barrier- free on a portion
- Store, cafe, playground, boat launch and rentals available
- Pets ok

Reservations, fees:
- Open all year, no reservations, $8/night, and $4/night for some primitive walk-in sites
- (206)687-4621 or Battle Ground Lake State Park, 17612 NE Palmer Road, Battle Ground, WA 98660

Site #21   CRESAP BAY PARK

Location: About 8 miles north of Vancouver on I-5 take the Fairground Exit 7 and drive 2 miles north to Duluth. Turn right and continue on State Route

502 for about 8 miles to the junction with State Route 503 at the traffic light at Battle Ground. Turn left (north) and continue on SR 503 through Amboy until you cross the Yale Bridge on the North Fork of the Lewis River. Proceed north on SR 503 for 0.5 mile to the campground entrance on the left.

Recommendation: A new campground and day use area with swimming and picnicking facilities opened in 1992. It's a very comfortable camp and can serve very conveniently for exploring the south side of the Monument.

Campsites, facilities:
- 58 campsites for tents or RV's of all lengths
- 15 group campsites with a shelter, fireplace, sink and electricity
- Piped water, flush toilets and showers
- RV sewage dump
- Boat launch and docks
- Pets ok on leash

Reservations, fees:
- Open Memorial Day through Labor Day, $8/night, no reservations
- Host on site
- (503)464-5024 or Pacific Power and Light Co., Recreation, 920 SW 6th Ave., Portland, OR 97204

WEST OF MOUNT ST. HELENS/SR 504 ACCESS

Site #22   SILVER LAKE MOTEL AND RESORT

Location: Take Exit 49 off I-5 and drive 6.5 miles on State Route 504 to the resort.

Recommendation: My first choice would be Seaquest State Park, but if you can't get in there try this one. It's on Silver Lake with a great view of Mount St. Helens. If you're into bass fishing this is one of the best spots in southwest WA. The new owners are extremely friendly and make you feel like part of the family.

Campsites, facilities:
- 11 tent sites and 22 sites for RV's of any length
- Piped water, flush toilets, showers, sewer hookups and electricity
- Store, ice and playground
- Food service within one mile
- Boat launching, docks and rentals and fishing tackle

- Pets on leash
- New owners with high interest in service
- Remodeled cabins and motel units built over the water

Reservations, fees:
- Open all year, $12.50/night for full hookup and $9.00/night for water and electricity, reservations
- Motel efficiency unit is $55.00/night and units with separate bedrooms are $70.00/night
- MasterCard, Visa and Discovery Card
- (206)274-6141 or Silver Lake Motel and Resort, 3201 Spirt Lake Highway, Silver Lake, WA 98645

Site #23   SEAQUEST STATE PARK

Location: Take Exit 49 off I-5 at Castle Rock and drive 5 miles east on SR 504 to the park.
Recommendation: This is the best possible camping opportunity if you're going to go to the visitor center or visit the Coldwater/Johnston Ridge area.
Campsites, facilities:
- 54 tent sites and 16 sites for RVs up to 50 ft
- Piped water, flush toilets, showers, sewer hookups and electricity
- Playground
- Wheelchair accessible
- Store within one mile

Reservations, fees:
- Open all year, $8/night, no reservations
- (206)274-8633 or Seaquest State Park, Box 3030, Spirit Lake Highway, Castle Rock, WA 98611

Site #24   VOLCANO VIEW RESORT

Location: Take Exit 49 off I-5 at Castle Rock and drive 9 miles east on SR 504 to the resort.
Recommendations: Although my preference is Seaquest State Park, this will do well if the park is full when you arrive. Bring along your fishing pole as this is some of the best bass fishing in the state.
Campsites, facilities:
- 15 tent sites and 26 full hookup sites for RV's of any length
- Piped water, sewer hookups and electricity

- Food service and ice
- Store, bottled gas and laundromat within 1 mile
- Boat docks, launch and rentals nearby
- Pets and motorbikes ok

Reservations, fees:

- Open all year, $12.50/night for full hookup and $10.00/night for water and electricity
- Reservations accepted, MasterCard and Visa
- (206)274-7087 or Volcano View Resort, 4220 Spirit Lake Highway, Silver Lake, WA 98645

Site #25   TOUTLE VILLAGE

Location: Take Exit 49 off I-5 at Castle Rock and drive 10 miles east on SR 504 to the park.

Recommendation: Although Seaquest is my first choice use this one if you're not able to get in, or if your main interest is fishing for bass.

Campsites, facilities:

- 10 drive-through sites for RV's of any length
- Piped water, showers, sewer hookups, electricity and flush toilets
- Food service, laundromat and ice
- Boat docks, launch and rentals nearby
- Pets and motorbikes ok

Reservations, fees:

- Open all year, $12/night, reservations

(206)274-6208 or Toutle Village, Toutle, WA 98649

NORTH OF MOUNT ST. HELENS/US 12 ACCESS

Site #26   IKE KINSAWA STATE PARK

Location: Take Exit 68 off I-5 and drive east on US 12 to Mossy Rock, the park is on Mayfield Lake.

Recommendation: This is a good spot if you have an RV and want to cool off around water. There's a lot to do, especially if you hike or have a boat.

Campsites, facilities:
- 60 tent sites and 41 sites for RV's up to 20 ft. long
- Piped water, flush toilets, sewer hookups, showers and electricity
- Food service, store and playground
- Wheelchair accessibility
- Boat docks and launch nearby
- Pets ok

Reservations, fees:
- Open all year, $8/night, reservations
- call (206)983-3402 or Ike Kinsawa State Park, 873 Harmony Road, Silver Creek, WA 98585

Site #27   LAKE MAYFIELD MARINA RESORT

Location: Take Exit 68 off I-5 and drive 15 miles east on US 12, then 1 mile south on Winston Road. It's on the shore of Mayfield Lake.

Recommendation: You're still a long way from the Mount St. Helens attractions at Road 99/Windy Ridge, but this is a large campground with lots to entertain the family.

Campsites, facilities:
- 50 tent sites and 100 full hookup sites for RV's of any length
- Piped water, sewer hookups, showers, flush toilets and electricity
- Food service, recreation hall, store and ice
- Laundromat within one mile
- Boat launch, docks, hiking and biking trails, and a riding stable nearby
- Pets ok

Reservations, fees:
- Open all year, $14.00/night for full hook-up
- (206)985-2357 or Lake Mayfield Marina Resort, 350 Hadaller, Mossy Rock, WA 98564

Site #28   HARMONY LAKESIDE RV PARK

Location: Take Exit 68 off I-5 and drive 18 miles east on US 12 and 2.5 miles north on Harmony Road.

Recommendation: A good location if the other campgrounds on Mayfield Lake are full.

Campsites, facilities:
- 28 tent sites with water and electricity and 48 full hookup sites for RV's of any length
- Piped water, sewer hookups, flush toilets, showers and electricity
- Some sites with cable TV
- Recreation hall and ice
- Boat docks and launch
- Pets and motorbikes ok

Reservations, fees:
- Open year round, $11/night for tents, $13/night with water and electricity, and $14/night with full hookup or $80/week
- Reservations, Good Sam
- MasterCard and Visa
- (206)983-3804 or Harmony Lakeside RV Park, 563 Harmony Road, Silver Creek, WA 98585

Site #29   REDMONDS RV PARK

Location: Take Exit 68 off I-5 and drive 50 miles east on US 12.
Recommendation: It's small but a good location for driving into the attractions on the north and east sides of the mountain.
Campsites, facilities:
- 10 tent sites and six full hookup sites for RV's of any length
- Piped water, sewer hookups, flush toilets and electricity
- Food service, store, bottled gas and ice
- Pets ok

Reservations, fees:
- Open all year, $12/night, reservations
- MasterCard, and Visa
- (206)498-5425 or Redmonds RV Park, 8136 US. Highway 12, Glenoma, WA 98336

Site #30   MAPLE GROVE CAMPGROUND AND RV PARK

Location: Take Exit 68 off I-5 and drive east on US 12 for about 52 miles to the town of Randle. Turn south on Forest Service Road 25 and drive 100 yards across the Cowlitz River to the park.

Recommendation: It's a convenient location but could be noisy so close to the main access road to the Monument. There is a helicopter tour to the Monument on site.

Campsites, facilities:
- six tent sites and 64 full hookup sites for RV's of any length
- Piped water, flush toilets, showers and electricity
- Food service, store, recreation hall, playground, laundromat, bottled gas and ice
- Pets ok

Reservations, fees:
- Open mid-April to December, $10/night, reservations
- (206)497-2741 or Maple Grove Campground and RV Park, P.O. Box 205, Randle, WA 98377

Site #31   PACKWOOD TRAILER AND RV PARK

Location: It's located in downtown Packwood on US 12.

Recommendation: It's a long way to the Mount St. Helens attractions but there are a lot of conveniences in this town.

Campsites, facilities:
- 20 tent sites and 66 full hookup sites for RV's of any length
- Piped water, sewer hookups, flush toilets, showers and electricity
- Store, bottled gas and ice
- Pets and motorbikes ok

Reservations, fees:
- Open all year, $14/night, or $10.00\night for tents with partial hookup, reservations
- MasterCard, Visa and Discovery Card
- (206)494-5145 or Packwood Trailer and RV Park, P.O. Box 309, Packwood, WA 98361

Site #32   OHANAPECOSH

Location: Take US 12 and SR 123 for 11 miles northeast of Packwood. The campground is next to the visitor center as you enter the Mount Rainier National Park.

Recommendation: This is a good camp if your plans include visiting Mount Rainier.

Campsites, facilities:
- 232 sites for tents or RV's up to 30 ft
- Piped water and flush toilets
- Some barrier-free
- Pets ok

Reservations, fees:
- Open mid-May to November, $5/night, no reservations
- (206)569-2211, or Mount Rainier National Park, Tahoma Woods, Ashford, WA 98304

Site #33   LA WIS WIS

Location: Take US 12 for seven miles northeast of Packwood and then Forest Service Road 1272, the campground entry road, for 0.5 mile west.

Recommendation: If you're traveling US 12 east of Packwood, this is the best camping opportunity on this side of White Pass.

Campsites, facilities:
- 110 sites for tents and RV's up to 30 ft
- Piped water, flush toilets and some vaults
- Pets ok

Reservations, fees:
- Open Memorial Day to September 30, $8 to $10/night, no reservations
- (206)494-5515 or Packwood Ranger District, 13068 US. Highway 12, Packwood, WA 98361

Site #34   IRON CREEK

Location: Take Forest Service Road 25 for 10 miles south of Randle.

Recommendation: This is the best campground for visiting the Road 99 viewpoints, especially if you're tenting or in a self-contained RV.

Campsites, facilities:
- 98 sites for tents or RV's up to 50 ft.
- Piped water and vault toilets
- Some barrier-free
- Interpretive trail on old-growth and an amphitheater for programs on weekends
- Pets ok

Reservations, fees:

- Open Memorial Day to September 30, $9/night for a single unit and $14/night for a double unit, extra vehicles are $3/night. You can make reservations through MISTIX Corporation by calling 1-800-283-CAMP. There is a non-refundable reservation fee of $6/family. In the event that this campground is full they will offer you space in two nearby Forest Service Campgrounds. Tower Rock Campground of 21 units is about five miles east on Road 76, and North Fork Campground of 32 units is about 10 miles east on Road 23. North Fork has three group sites that can handle up to 40 people.
- (206)497-7565 or Randle Ranger District, Randle, WA 98377

Site #35 TOWER ROCK RV PARK AND CAMPGROUND

Location: Take Road 25 south from US 12 at Randle for about 10 miles to Iron Creek Campground, turn east on Road 76 and drive 5 miles to the campground.

Recommendation: If the Forest Service campground at Iron Creek is full this is a good opportunity as you're close to the volcano viewpoints. You can pay to fish at about $2.50 per pound. The poles and bait are provided. There is no license required.

Campsites, facilities:

- 21 beautiful wooded campsites and numerous primitive sites
- Trailer dump site and flush toilets
- Playfield and equipment
- Bike rentals, groceries and gas

Reservations, fees:

- Open all year, $8.00/night for a tent site, $10.00/night for electric and water, and $12.00/night for full hookup
- Call (206) 497-7680 or Tower Rock RV Park and Campground, 137 Cispus Drive, Randle, WA 98377

Mount St. Helens Visitor Center at Silver Lake is the best place to obtain information for helping you discover this fascinating Monument.

Guided Tours and other Services

Bus Tours

If you are confident to drive on the forest roads described in this book, you should be able to follow most of the main pathways and discover most of the Monument. Some of you may be uneasy about driving on mountain roads and would prefer to leave the driving to someone else. I often search out a guided bus tour when I travel to a new city and find it to be the quickest way to see and learn the most about that city. There are several qualified van and bus tours that have permits to operate within the Mount St. Helens National Volcanic Monument. The following tour services have permits and meet federal standards and carry adequate liability insurance.

Guided Tour	Type of Vehicle
Cowlitz Valley Tours 129 Young Road Randle, WA 98377 (206) 497-2731	15 passenger van 1 trip per day
Evergreen Stage Line, Inc. P.O. Box 17306 Portland, OR 97217 (503) 285-9845	Standard bus Charters
Encore Northwest Excursions 168 Landie Rd. Randle, WA 98377 (206) 497-2600	15 passenger van Charters
Good Time Chariot Travel Club 12128 Cyprus Way Suite A-100 Mukilteo, WA 98275 (206) 778-1414	Tour bus Seniors

Grayline of Seattle   Standard bus
720 S Forest   Charters
Seattle, WA 98134
(206) 624-5077

Mount St. Helens Adventure Tours   10 passenger van
920 Schaffon Rd.
Castle Rock, WA 98611
(206) 274-6542 or (800) 756-0243

Raz Transportation   Standard bus
1600 SW Bertha Blvd.   Charters
Portland, OR 97219
(503) 246-3301

Whitney's Van Excursions   15 passenger van
123 Pioneer Road   Charters
Montesano, WA 98563
(206) 249-4431 or 532-5818

Aerial Tours

The area impacted by the lateral blast is so vast that it is difficult to appreciate the size from the ground. There are many aerial tours available from airports around the perimeter of the Monument and you'll see several helicopter services operating along the travel routes to the Monument. You'll find that it cost more per hour for the helicopters than a fixed wing plane. The helicopters are able to fly over the area in shorter time because they are based closer. You'll fly slower in the helicopter and will see more.

The helicopter flights cost about $65 to $85 per person but you usually need to have three or four persons in the aircraft. The fixed wing airplanes cost about $35 to $50 per person with a minimum of three people. The airports at Chehalis, WA and Troutdale, OR are approved by the Federal Aviation Administration for these types of flights.

References

USDA Forest Service. 1989 edition "Mount St. Helens National Monument, Recreation Opportunity Guide", Gifford Pinchot National Forest, Vancouver, WA   41 pp.

USDA Forest Service. October 1985 "Mount St. Helens National Volcanic Monument, Final Environmental Impact Statement, Comprehensive Management Plan", Gifford Pinchot National Forest, Vancouver, WA 450 pp.

USDA Forest Service. January 1992 "Four Year Program for the Mount St. Helens National Volcanic Monument, 1992-1995", Gifford Pinchot National Forest, Vancouver, WA   30 pp.

USDI Geological Survey. "Eruptions of Mount St. Helens: Past, Present, and Future", by Robert I. Tilling   46 pp.

USDI Geological Survey. 1982 "Volcanic Eruptions of 1980 at Mount St. Helens, The First 100 Days", by Foxworthy and Hill, Geological Survey Professional Paper 1249,   125 pp.

US Army Corps of Engineers. 1990 "Mount St. Helens Recovery", GPO 1990-793-159,   12 pp.

USDI Geological Survey. November 2, 1992 issue of Earthquakes & Volcanoes, Volume 23, "Small Explosions Interrupt 3-Year Quiescence at Mount St. Helens, Washington", by Myers, Cascade Volcano Observatory, 16 pp.

USDI Geological Survey. October 1992 "Volcanic Hazards, Mount St. Helens" draft report by the Cascade Volcano Observatory, Vancouver, WA 10 pp.

Weyerhaeuser Co.. 1992 "Mount St. Helens, Weyerhaeuser's Reforestation" brochure by Weyerhaeuser Company, Tacoma, WA

KC Publications, Inc. 1985   "Mount St. Helens, The Story Behind The Scenery", by Corcoran   48 pp.

Emergency telephones are strategically located throughout the Monument.

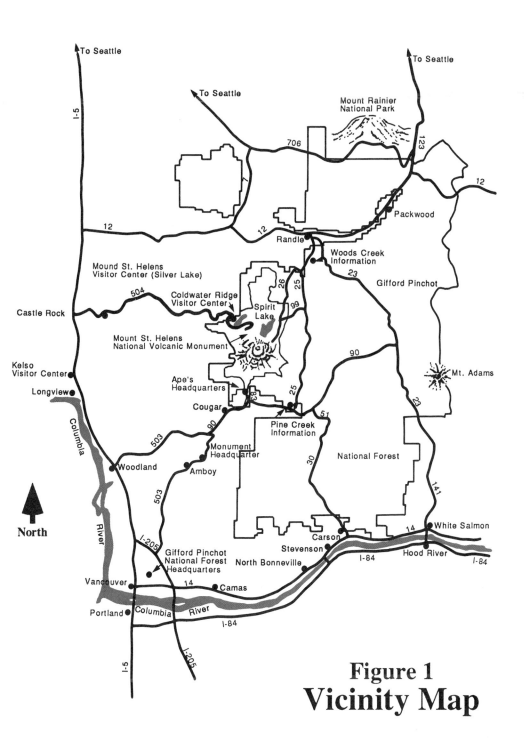

Figure 1
Vicinity Map

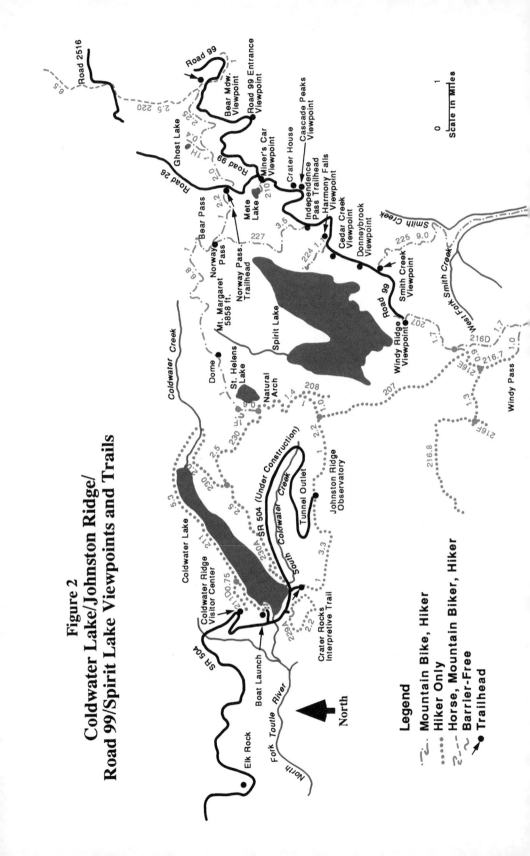

Figure 2
Coldwater Lake/Johnston Ridge/
Road 99/Spirit Lake Viewpoints and Trails

Scale in Miles

0   1

Legend

·ı·ı· Mountain Bike, Hiker

····· Hiker Only

~ı~ı~ Horse, Mountain Biker, Hiker

⟨ Barrier-Free

● Trailhead

North

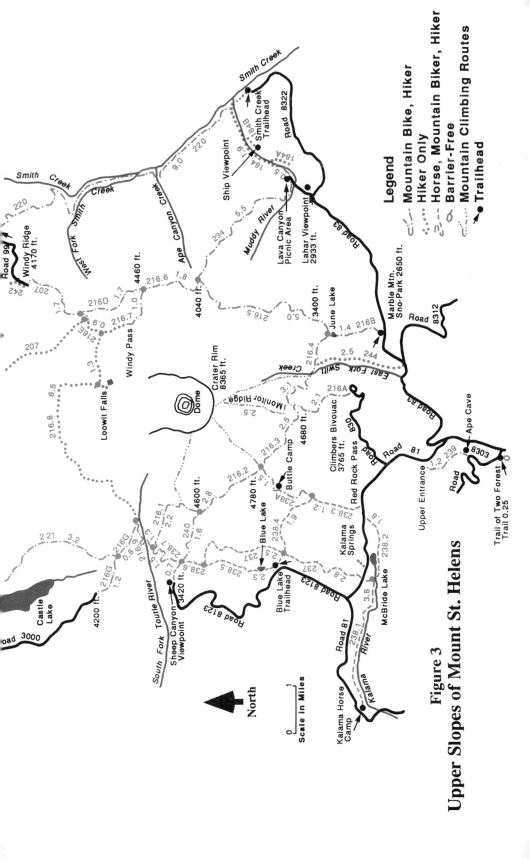

Figure 3
Upper Slopes of Mount St. Helens

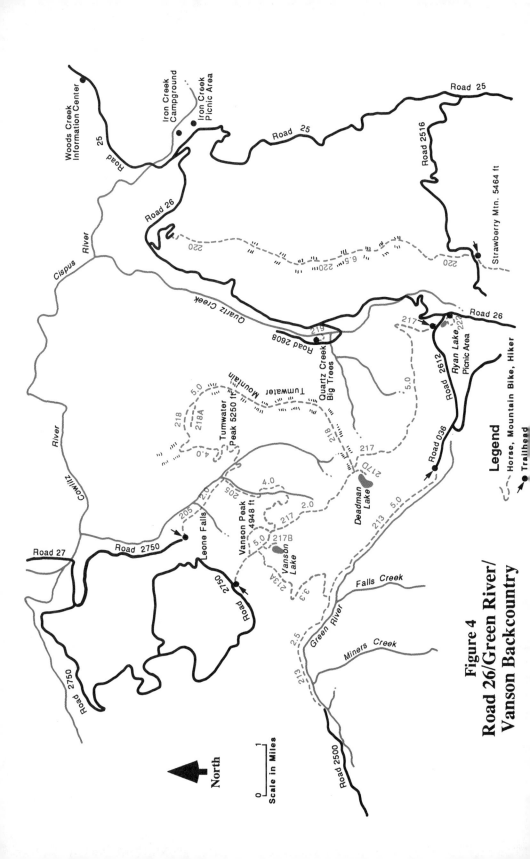

Figure 4
**Road 26/Green River/
Vanson Backcountry**

Figure 5
Lewis River Falls Area

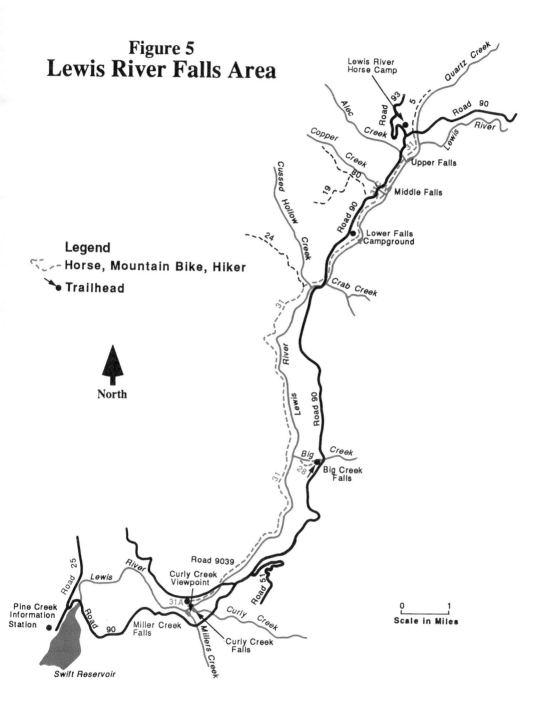

Legend
- Horse, Mountain Bike, Hiker
- Trailhead

North

Scale in Miles
0   1

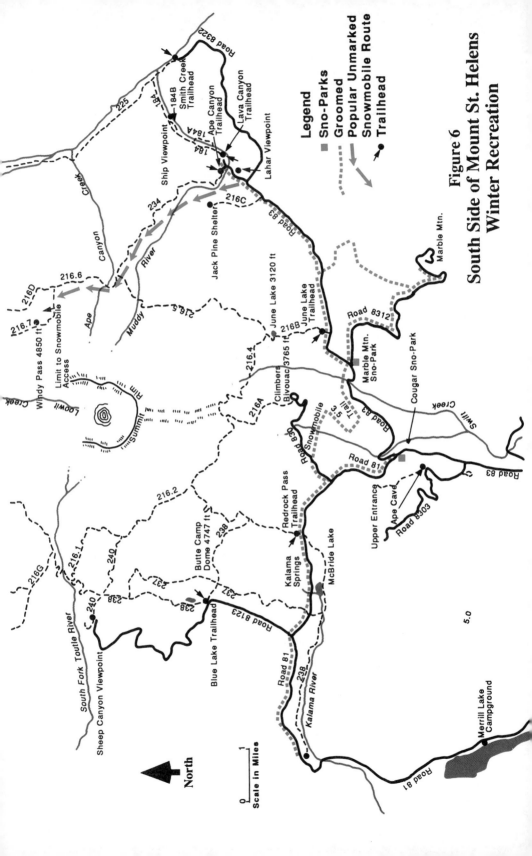

Figure 6

South Side of Mount St. Helens Winter Recreation

Legend

■ Sno-Parks

Groomed

Popular Unmarked Snowmobile Route

● Trailhead

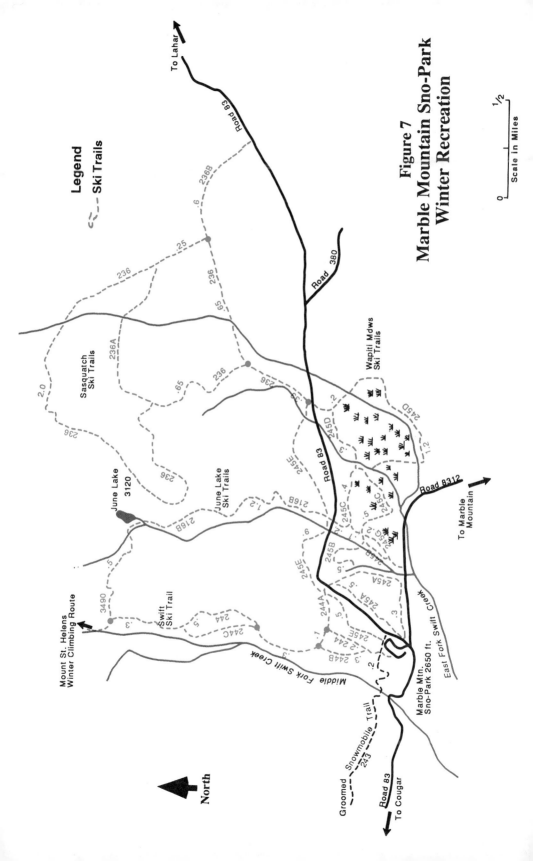

Figure 7
Marble Mountain Sno-Park
Winter Recreation

Order from: A Plus Images, 4519 NE 49th St., Vancouver, WA 98661 or call (206) 694-6356

Additional copies:

Mount St. Helens, Pathways to Discovery	$14.95/copy
Shipping and handling: Book rate, takes 3 to 4 weeks	$1.50/first
2 day mail service	$3.00/copy
WA. state residents add 7.6% sales tax.	$1.14/copy

Buy more than one and I'll pay the shipping.

Free Brochures

Send the names of your friends that are interested in Mount St. Helens and I'll send them a free brochure about the book.

Photographs

All of the photographs displayed in this book are available in prints up to 16 in. x 20 in., either framed or unframed as souvenirs of your trip. Frames are light oak with a mat. Request photos by page number. Prices are :

Photo Size	Color Unframed	Color Framed	B & W Unframed	B & W Framed
8 X 10	$14.95	$24.95	$9.95	$19.95
11 X 14	$19.95	$29.95	$14.95	$24.95
16 X 20	$29.95	$39.95	$24.95	$34.95

WA state residents add 7.6 % sales tax.
Add $3.00 shipping and handling.

Speaking Engagements

The author has produced several audiovisual programs on the Mount St. Helens eruptions and recreation planning and is available as a speaker. For local service organizations there is no fee if he is allowed to sell the book. For conventions and seminars the fee varies with audience size and travel expense.

Dave is also available as a step-on guide with Greyline Tours. For information call (800) 422-7042.